STREETS RIPE FOR HARVEST

Empowering the church to take
the gospel to the streets

John Caldwell

"Some wish to live within the sound of church or chapel bell; I want to run a Rescue Shop within a yard of hell."

C.T. STUDD

CONTENTS

Title Page
Epigraph
Acknowledgements
Endorsements — 4
Introduction — 6
Chapter One: You are a missionary and the streets are your mission field — 11
Chapter Two: Are you gripped by the one true gospel? — 16
Chapter Three: Re-aligning our motives: a vision of God's glory — 24
Chapter Four: Streets ripe for harvest: catching the vision of Jesus — 32
Chapter Five: Taking the kingdom to the streets — 39
Chapter Six: Street encounters — 45
Chapter Seven: Sowing and reaping — 52
Chapter Eight: Street ministry is team ministry — 57
Chapter Nine: Anointing: the source of impact and authority — 62
Final thoughts: hear the call, feel the call, obey — 67

the call

Appendices   69

Appendix 1: "A Vision of the Lost" by William   70
Booth

Appendix 2: How to Become Fishers of Men by   79
Charles Spurgeon

ACKNOWLEDGEMENTS

Thanks are due to many folks for their encouragement in this project. Specific thanks are due to Liz Dobson for her eagle-eyed editing. Thank you to Alistair Matheson for not only his endorsement, but also the helpful feedback on the manuscript. To all who provided a written endorsement: thank you!

Streets Ripe for Harvest

Empowering the church to take
the gospel to the streets

John Caldwell

© 2022 John Caldwell

ENDORSEMENTS

Wow! Who knew such a little book could carry so much dynamite in its pages. I know John practises what he shares in these pages because I actually met him while he was out doing it several times many years ago. Get ready to be challenged, compelled to come out of your comfort zone and expect to be revitalised in your passion for sharing Jesus on the streets where you live.

Craig Denham, Pastor at Love Church

An important work and a highly motivational read! Christians and non-Christians alike have been turned away and switched off by 'street preaching' that isn't the best advert for Jesus. But the adage stands: the solution to misuse is not disuse but proper use. Holy Spirit-anointed preaching has never been replaced by anything superior – it has never lost the power to draw people to Jesus on the streets. Conversely, harsh rhetoric has never lost the knack of turning people cold inside church buildings either.

John Caldwell reminds us, with irresistible reason, why Jesus has never stopped sending His disciples onto the streets: We are called to reach people, and the streets are filled with people. John writes with the flow of the anointed preacher that he himself is, his narrative engaging, disarming and compelling. Thank God for three things Jesus has supplied us with: a wonderful Gospel, the enablement of the Spirit, and mobilisers like John to ignite us to action. There's surely no better time than post-lockdown for the church collectively to resolve: Let's get out there!

Alistair Matheson, author of 'The Big Picture: God's Plan for Everything' and several other books, Pastor of Glasgow City Church, and member of the National Leadership Team of the Apostolic Church UK

Streets Ripe for Harvest is powerful, timely and relevant book from John Caldwell. A must read for those with a heart to see Jesus in action out with the four walls of a church building. This book challenges to us to ask ourselves: are we living out the Christian life in our comfort zone; are we in the western church mired in 'the culture of blindness' oblivious of those in need all around us; and are we truly proclaiming Christ to the lost by both witness and words? A riveting read for anyone with a genuine passion for revival, renewal and restoration.

Colin Murray - Pastor of Portsoy Community Church and author of 'Papering over the Cracks'

INTRODUCTION

Why do we not see more people saved today? Why are there not more signs and wonders being manifest through the body of Christ? Why is there a lack of life, vibrancy, and power in much of what goes by the name 'church'? I believe the answer is simple. The gospel was never intended to be contained within the four walls of a church building. The gospel was given for the streets because the streets are where people are.

Take a walk through your nearest town or city and ask the Holy Spirit to help you see what he sees. If you do this you will be amazed at what you never saw before. Our streets are filled with the broken, the depressed and the addicted. Our streets are full of people with empty hearts. They might be down and out, or up and out, they may be lying in the gutter, or strutting along in their Armani suit, but the emptiness is there. They need the hope of the gospel, but if you or I never connect with them, they will never hear about the hope that can be theirs.

> How, then, can they call on the one they have not believed in? And how can they believe in the one of whom they have not heard? And how can they hear without someone preaching to them? And how can anyone preach unless they are sent? As it is written: "How beautiful are the feet of those who bring good

news!"

(Romans 10:14-15)

Darkness fills our streets. Prostitution happens on the streets. Drug dealing takes place on the streets. Violence explodes on the streets – if there is anywhere on earth that the gospel of Jesus Christ is needed it's the streets.

Whilst our churches are singing praises in the comforts of our contemporary cathedrals, people walking past our church buildings are dying and going to hell. This call to take the gospel to the streets is one of most neglected commands of Jesus Christ: "And then he told them, 'Go into all the world and preach the Good News to everyone.'" Mark 16:15 (NLT) Jesus said "Go!" Go where? To the people. And where are the people? On the streets.

When we take the gospel to the streets, we create an opportunity for the Holy Spirit to manifest his love and power through us. One of the reasons why the anointing that we experience on Sunday, wears off by Monday, is because we are not giving it away throughout the week. In my experience, whenever I have taken the gospel to the streets, God does the unexpected. Divine appointments take place. People receive prayer. Sick people are healed. Folks feel the presence of God. The anointing wasn't intended to be consumed, it is given to be passed on: "Freely you have received; freely give." (Matt 10:8) Many church goers are like the Dead Sea, there are rivers of blessing flowing into them, but there is no outlet. When this happens the life we have received becomes death. Nothing grows because there is no outworking of God's grace.

I've been a Christian since 1999. From the moment I was born again, the Lord placed a burden on my heart for the streets. Since the moment I was saved, I saw the streets through new eyes – the eyes of Christ. God wants you to see things this way too. For some reason, followers of Jesus like hanging around Jesus, but not all of us are able to see the things that Jesus wants us to see: "Don't you have a saying, 'It's still four months until harvest'? I tell you, open your eyes and look at the fields! They are ripe for harvest." (John 4:35)

That verse is the inspiration for this book. The streets are ripe for harvest! You and I just need the spiritual vision to see what Christ sees. How does that happen? If you listen to many believers today, you will hear some say that it is a question of training, or skills, or life experience, or "gifting" – whilst all these factors have a role to play, I don't believe any of these are the starting point.

The starting point is the heart. We need to allow God to touch our hearts. We must run after His heart. As we allow our hearts to reflect His heart, we will begin to see with fresh vision. We don't see the harvest primarily with our physical eyes, we see the harvest through our spiritual eyes: the eyes of our heart. In Ephesians 1, Paul prays for "the eyes of your hearts" to be enlightened, that you may know." As we wrestle in prayer with God, and as we ask him to soften our hearts, open our eyes, hear his call and to feel what he feels we must be prepared to be ruined on the altar.

We run from this kind of calling yet the reality is this is Christianity 101. A heart for the lost is not advanced level Christian living, it ought to be basic Christian living. How can we live comfortably knowing Jesus shed His blood for masses of people who have never heard about his saving grace? How can we be satisfied knowing that people will not be saved unless they hear the gospel, repent and believe? How can we glorify God in our worship knowing that countless others have yet to discover the purpose they were created: to glorify God and to enjoy Him forever.

We must fall to our knees. Before we speak to people on the streets, we must cry to God on our knees. Before we proclaim his goodness in public, we must pour out our hearts to him in private. If we are earnest, he will touch us with the sacred flame of heaven.

> O Thou who camest from above,
> the pure celestial fire to impart
> kindle a flame of sacred love
> upon the mean altar of my heart.

Let us begin here. Before you read any further, join with me in praying to the Father for fresh fire. Let's ask Him to touch our hearts and open our eyes, that we may see the need and hear the call and that we may have boldness to "Go!"

CHAPTER ONE: YOU ARE A MISSIONARY AND THE STREETS ARE YOUR MISSION FIELD

"Come, follow me," Jesus said, "and I will send you out to fish for people." (Matt 4:19)

"Every Christian is either a missionary or an impostor."
Charles Spurgeon

Every Christian is called to be a missionary. Jesus said to his disciples: "Peace be with you! As the Father has sent me, I am sending you." (John 20:21) The word mission simply means "to send". God is a missionary God. He is a sending God. He has revealed himself by sending his Son, and his Son in turn calls us to himself and then sends us out. Believers in Christ have been given the Holy Spirit, and the Holy Spirit is a missionary. Henry Martyn once said: 'The Spirit of Christ is the spirit of missions. The nearer we get to him, the more intensely missionary we become.' This is true. Jesus himself said: "But you will receive power when the Holy Spirit comes on you; and you will be my witnesses in Jerusalem, and in all Judea and Samaria, and to the ends of the earth." (Acts 1:8) One of the primary purposes of the Baptism with the Holy Spirit, is that the church – you and me – would be empowered for mission. To be a witness for Christ in the various spheres he has called us is our mandate; the empowering presence of God is the means by which we accomplish that mandate.

Being called to be a missionary means we are called to reach people. Yet many Christians live lives in isolation from unbelievers. If they work in a secular environment, they box their faith away on Sunday night, and open it up again for the following Sunday morning. Their primary social activities are with other Christians, and there are very few non-Christians in the lives of many professing Christians. For many professing believers, they are family Christians. They are in church because it is what their family do. Many I'm sure are sincere, but it sincerely falls short of New Testament Christianity. The western church, by and large, has become a religious middle-class social bubble. The call to missions, is the call to break out of this bubble.

The early church actually had the same problem. After Pentecost, the outpouring of the Spirit resulted in mass conversions of Jewish people. Jewish people were discovering faith in Christ as the Messiah. The Jerusalem church was thriving, but it was quickly becoming a religious ghetto. The apostles were not leading the great commission as they were supposed to, instead they were filling seats of influence and power. They were caught up in church. God had to do two things to burst the bubble. The first thing he did was allow persecution to break out. This led to the church being scattered – consequently the scattered church began to share their faith as they travelled. The second thing God did was to raise up a new apostle, one who would take the gospel beyond the comfortable walls of Jerusalem.

The same thing is starting to happen in the West. Whilst we know nothing of the kind of persecution that the early Christians who suffered under Rome encountered, nor do we know the sufferings, imprisonment, and martyrdom that is experienced by brothers and sisters in other parts of the world – the West is changing and it's changing fast. The gospel of Christ is increasingly unwelcome. Don't believe me? Stand in the streets of London and read the book of Romans out loud and you will likely fuel a mob which will draw the attention of the police, and you will be charged and taken away by the police. It doesn't matter that the charges will be eventually dropped because there has been a breach of your legal rights, the default position is to silence the preaching, and arrest the preacher.

In one sense, this is a good thing that is happening. It wasn't too long ago that the gospel met with complete indifference. Twenty years ago, when I first started preaching on the streets, many people would walk by without batting an eyelid. Now, if you preach even the most gracious and loving gospel message, there is still every chance you will spark a hostile reaction. People will yell all sorts of absurdities and blasphemies at you. People will tell you that you are not welcome to preach the gospel in *their* town. People will be agitated by your presence and your message. We need to understand the spiritual dynamic that is at work here. There are forces of darkness at work, and they are working overtime to baptise everyone in darkness and unbelief. Their campaign is gaining momentum, but the gospel is an assault on the kingdom of darkness. "For our struggle is not against flesh and blood, but against the rulers, against the authorities, against the powers of this dark world and against the spiritual forces of evil in the heavenly realms." (Eph 6:12)

Many Christians will agree with my premise that every Christian is a missionary, but they will disagree that the streets are our mission field. Instead they will say that our families are our mission field, or our work place, or our places of leisure (gyms, clubs, and places of interest). These *are* also our mission fields, but *so are the streets*. Aside from the many scriptural examples of street ministry (Old Testament prophets, John the Baptist, Jesus and the apostles all preached in the open-air) the reason you are called to the streets is because this is where people are. People both live and pass through streets. The streets are the market place. The streets are the place of exchange. Small businesses set up their stalls in the streets, buskers sing and perform in the streets, political parties' campaign in the streets, young people hang about the streets, rough sleepers beg on the streets, drug dealers deal on the streets – life happens on the streets. The streets are full of people, opportunities and encounters – more than ever we need to bring light, hope and the word of faith into the streets. The streets are full of desperate people, deceived people, and distracted people. The streets showcase every other consumerist preacher—Apple, McDonald's, River Island – and multitudes of other brands proclaim their product from bus stops, digital bill-boards and shop windows. They draw people with their promise of satisfaction, yet emptiness remains. Consumerism is a cheap altar to worship at. The streets are an intersection and interchange of people, products, and encounter – and the gospel of the Kingdom needs to be seen and heard in this fertile mission ground.

The heart of the missionary is to reach lost people, and our streets have herds of lost people. Why would we not take the gospel to the streets?

CHAPTER TWO: ARE YOU GRIPPED BY THE ONE TRUE GOSPEL?

I am astonished that you are so quickly deserting him who called you in the grace of Christ and are turning to a different gospel. (Gal 1:6)

"Jesus is not one of many ways to approach God, nor is He the best of several ways; He is the only way." A.W. Tozer

One of the realities that has struck me over the 21 or so years that I've been a Christian, is the confusion surrounding the nature of the gospel. Just what exactly is the gospel? You'd think that was a simple question, but it's not. Centuries of religious tradition, theological liberalism, and a myriad of social gospels have left many Christians in a state of confusion and ineffectiveness. It's my conviction that this loss of the gospel is one of the reasons why many professing Christians are not engaged in mission and it's one of the primary reasons why very few believers are motivated to take the gospel to the streets – they don't know the true gospel, and they haven't encountered its power at work in their own souls.

Closely paralleling this issue is the challenge of secular culture. Many present day professing Christians spent their childhood in Sunday school colouring in pictures of Noah's Ark, and their adolescence in church youth groups being told they were a 'history maker' and their adult church-life listening to seeker-sensitive sermonettes that have watered down the preaching of the gospel to the point where the message is crossless, Christless, and powerless. Whilst the church has been repackaging itself in shallow euphemisms, the moral worldview of Christians has been shaped by a belief system that has been far more active and effective in making disciples: secular humanism has been shaping the minds and hearts of the nation through education, government legislation, and media. In other words, the church has abandoned discipleship, and the world has taken up the mantle. The reason why we are so weak in mission and discipleship is simply because the world has been more effective in reaching us than we have been at reaching the world.

We have failed to embody the foundational message of Paul: "Do not be conformed to this world, but be transformed by the renewing of your mind, that you may prove what is that good and acceptable and perfect will of God." (Rom 12:2) The word "world" here means the values and desires of this fallen world. Paul is telling us not to be shaped by the world's philosophy and values and thinking. Instead we are to be transformed by the renewal of our mind. Our natural way of thinking is defined by our fallen nature. This world reflects the values and thinking of fallen people. The gospel is God-centred, the world is human-centred. That is why humanism is the natural religion of this world. Humanism at its core is anti-God.

The apostle John also reinforces this truth:

> Do not love the world or anything in the world. If anyone loves the world, the love of the Father is not in him. For all that is in the world—the desires of the flesh, the desires of the eyes, and the pride of life—is not from the Father but from the world. The world is passing away, along with its desires; but whoever does the will of God remains forever. (1 John 2:15-17)

John goes on to talk about the spirit of deception. He makes it clear that the world is not only shaped by fallen nature, it is also shaped by seductive spirits who are deceiving billions of people. John says:

> By this you will know the Spirit of God: Every spirit that confesses that Jesus Christ has come in the flesh is from God, and every spirit that does not confess Jesus is not from God. This is the spirit of the antichrist, which you have heard is coming and which is already in the world at this time.
>
> You, little children, are from God and have overcome them, because greater is He who is in you than he who is in the world. They are of the world. That is why they speak from the world's perspective, and the world listens to them. We are from God. Whoever knows God listens to us; whoever is not from God does not listen to us. That is how we know the Spirit of truth and the spirit of deception. (1 John 4:2-6)

When the church of Jesus Christ allows herself to be conformed into the world's way of thinking, she adopts attitudes, values and beliefs that are resistant to the truth of God. If a genuine believer in Christ becomes steeped in the world's values, and neglects the mind of the Spirit, that Christian will find themselves working against God's purposes, even though on the surface they may look religious. One of the places I found to be the most-anti-evangelism was an interdenominational theological college. Despite having a reputation for being invested in international mission, this college and many of its students were so conditioned by humanism that the simple prospect of preaching the gospel was an offense to them. As a new Christian, during class discussion, I'd often bring up the subject of evangelism only to be shot down in flames. 21 years later, I've observed the same anti-evangelism traits in many professing Christians. There is something about religion that hates the gospel of Jesus Christ.

The irony is, the very thing the religious and worldly church despises, is the very thing that will deliver it out of its spiritual slumber. The gospel of Jesus Christ. The gospel is not only the answer for the lost, it is the answer for a backslidden and apostate church. Throughout church history whenever some soul has caught gospel fire in their belly, and dared to preach the true gospel in the power of the Spirit, the dead wood in the pews and the presbyteries get shaken afresh by the power of the Spirit. The results are catalytic. It results in either revival or resistance but never indifference. The worldly church recognises the subversive power of the gospel and will fight it at all costs – just like the religious mafia at the time of Jesus and the apostles.

The call to the mission field that is the streets is essential, but just as essential is the nature of the gospel we carry. Only the true gospel can meet the needs of the streets. Only the true gospel will radiate the spiritual authority that will be needed to overcome the demonic atmosphere that permeates many of our streets and cities. Only the true gospel will lead hearers to an encounter with Jesus Christ and only the true gospel will set the captives free.

How do we know what the true gospel is? It's simple: we look to the scriptures. What does the Old Testament say about the ministry of Jesus? What did John the Baptist say? What did Jesus himself teach and do? What message did the apostles preach?

When we study these questions in light of the whole of scripture, a clear picture emerges. We see God in the flesh, dying for sin, rising again, and ascending on high. We see a call to repentance, warnings of a future judgement, and a promise of eternal life.

Look at the first post-ascension message that was preached by the apostle Peter on the day of Pentecost:

> Listen to this: Jesus of Nazareth was a man ac-

> credited by God to you by miracles, wonders and signs, which God did among you through him, as you yourselves know. This man was handed over to you by God's deliberate plan and foreknowledge; and you, with the help of wicked men, put him to death by nailing him to the cross. But God raised him from the dead, freeing him from the agony of death, because it was impossible for death to keep its hold on him.... "Repent and be baptized, every one of you, in the name of Jesus Christ for the forgiveness of your sins. And you will receive the gift of the Holy Spirit. The promise is for you and your children and for all who are far off—for all whom the Lord our God will call." (Acts 2)

This message is not some culturally bound, 'relevant for then' but 'not now' part of scripture. This message is the essence of the gospel of Jesus Christ. Peter is preaching the person of Jesus Christ, his death and resurrection and he is boldly calling his hearers to repent and receive the Holy Spirit.

The liberal gospel of socialism has morphed into the present cultural Marxist humanist worldview that worships at the altar of "inclusion" and "equality". 21st century people seem to have short memories though. It's a communist kind of equality. An equality that comes at the cost of diversity, freedom and true pluralism. This kind of thinking has seeped into our gospel messages. We now believe a gospel that offends no one, confronts no one and saves no one because to even suggest that people need to be saved is to be guilty of discrimination. God loves everyone and accepts everyone as they are – this is the God of paganism and the apostate western church.

The God of scripture, on the other hand, is a Holy God. He is a reigning, majestic King. He is a God who will share his glory with no one else. He rules and he reigns and he loves us deeply and passionately. His love was expressed through the cross of Jesus.

Jesus died as a substitute for the sinner. He was guiltless, we are guilty. Because we have broken God's laws and rejected his Word, we are all by default condemned. Religion cannot save anyone. Trying to be good won't get anyone in to heaven. We have been sold as slaves to our sinful ways. A ransom price needed to be paid, and Jesus paid that ransom with the only thing that could atone for our sin: his precious blood.

People don't just need a bit of religion. Praying and trying to be kinder is not the essence of Christianity. The human condition is so thoroughly evil that the only way any of us could be saved was for God himself to stand in the gap. The Word (God the Son) became flesh and allowed himself to be shredded by whip (embedded with bones) at the hands of a Roman guard. He suffered public humiliation. He had a crown of thick, giant thorns forced into his skull. He was spat on. His beard was plucked from his face. They punched him and kicked him and forced him to carry his own cross to the place of his execution. He was then nailed, hands and feet, to the cross and left to die. On the cross he took the fullness of God's wrath. God punished Jesus on our behalf. All who trust in Jesus are now saved from the wrath of God because Jesus paid the price in full. All who reject Jesus will face the wrath of God on their own, and they will be condemned to hell for eternity. This is the gospel.

CHAPTER THREE: RE-ALIGNING OUR MOTIVES: A VISION OF GOD'S GLORY

For the earth will be filled with the knowledge of the glory of the LORD as the waters cover the sea. (Hab 2:14)

"Missions is not the ultimate goal of the Church. Worship is. Missions exists because worship doesn't. Worship is ultimate, not missions, because God is ultimate, not man. When this age is over, and the countless millions of the redeemed fall on their faces before the throne of God, missions will be no more. It is a temporary necessity. But worship abides forever." John Piper

It's not only important to know what our message is – we need to be clear on the motivation. There are all sorts of faulty motivations for serving God in mission. Pride can be a motivation – this is what the Pharisees were guilty of. They liked to do their deeds of kindness and religion to look good before their peers. We can fall prey to this too. Perhaps we want church leaders and other believers to think we are sold out for God. We are more in love with the image of being a devoted Christian than we are the reality of being a devoted follower.

Guilt can also be a false motivation. I know some churches that seem to have implemented evangelistic excellence. Their people are out witnessing regularly. They do street work, door-to-door, and many other forms of evangelism – it looks good but there is a fly in the ointment: the people are motivated by guilt and fear. They are afraid of going to hell, or they are afraid of not going to heaven, so they slavishly hope to get God's (and their leaders') approval by doing all the right things.

However, even good motivations, if not balanced by the primary motivation, can lead us to a skewed missional motivation. For example, the fact that people are lost without Christ and headed to hell unless they repent of their sins *should* cause us to feel compassion. The physical suffering of those without adequate natural resources, or those who are sleeping rough, or the anguish of those who are drowning in addiction should cause us to respond empathetically. However, compassion for the lost and the suffering, on its own is not enough. We need a higher motivation. We need to be motivated by the glory of God!

Paris Reidhead powerfully demonstrates this principle in his watershed sermon, *Ten Shekels and a Shirt*.

> If you'll ask me why I went to Africa, I'll tell you I went primarily to improve on the justice of God. I didn't think it was right for anybody to go to Hell without a chance to be saved. So I went to give poor sinners a chance to go to heaven. Now I hadn't put it in so many words, but if you'll analyze what I just told you do you know what it is? Humanism. That I

STREETS RIPE FOR HARVEST

was simply using the provisions of Jesus Christ as a means to improve upon human conditions of suffering and misery... I went out there motivated by humanism. I'd seen pictures of lepers, I'd seen pictures of ulcers, I'd seen pictures of native funerals, and I didn't want my fellow human beings to suffer in Hell eternally after such a miserable existence on earth. But it was there in Africa that God began to tear THROUGH THE OVERLAY OF THIS HUMANISM! ... There alone in my bedroom AS I FACED GOD HONESTLY WITH WHAT MY HEART FELT, it seemed to me I heard Him say, "Yes, will not the Judge of all the earth do right? The Heathen are lost. And they're going to go to Hell, not because they haven't heard the gospel. They're going to go to Hell because they are sinners, WHO LOVE THEIR SIN! And because they deserve Hell. BUT, I didn't send you out there for them. I didn't send you out there for their sakes." And I heard as clearly as I've ever heard, though it wasn't with physical voice but it was the echo of truth of the ages finding its way into an open heart. I heard God say to my heart that day something like this, "I didn't send you to Africa for the sake of the heathen, I sent you to Africa for My sake. They deserved Hell! But I LOVE THEM!!! AND I ENDURED THE AGONIES OF HELL FOR THEM!!! I DIDN'T SEND YOU OUT THERE FOR THEM!!! I SENT YOU OUT THERE FOR ME! DO I NOT DESERVE THE REWARD OF MY SUFFERING? DON'T I DESERVE THOSE FOR WHOM I DIED?"

Hear those words: "I didn't send you out there for them!!! I sent you out there for me! *Do I not deserve the reward of my suffering*? Don't I deserve those for whom I died?" Jesus shed his blood to purchase men and women from every tribe, tongue and nation. When he went to the cross, he didn't see salvation from hell as the end-game – he looked forward to the fullness of redemption: a glorified and redeemed people of God.

Reidhead again, in that flesh-slaying sermon, illustrates this point:

> Two young Moravians heard of an island in the West Indies where an atheist British owner had 2000 to 3000 slaves. And the owner had said, "No preacher, no clergyman, will ever stay on this island. If he's ship wrecked we'll keep him in a separate house until he has to leave, but he's never going to talk to any of us about God, I'm through with all that nonsense." Three thousand slaves from the jungles of Africa brought to an island in the Atlantic and there to live and die without hearing of Christ.
>
> Two young Moravians heard about it. They sold themselves to the British planter and used the money they received from their sale, for he paid no more than he would for any slave, to pay their passage out to his island for he wouldn't even transport them. As the ship left its pier in the river at Hamburg and was going out into the North Sea carried with the tide, the Moravians had come from Herrnhut to see these two lads off, in their early twenties. Never to return again, for this wasn't a four year term, they sold themselves into life time slavery. Simply that as slaves, they could be as Christians where these others were. The families were there weeping, for they knew they would never see them again. And they wondered why they were going and questioned the wisdom of it. As the gap widened and the hous-

ings had been cast off and were being curled up there on the pier, and the young boys saw the widening gap, one lad with his arm linked through the arm of his fellow, raised his hand and shouted across the gap the last words that were heard from them, they were these, "MAY THE LAMB THAT WAS SLAIN RECEIVE THE REWARD OF HIS SUFFERING!" This became the call of Moravian missions. And this is the only reason for being: **That the Lamb that was slain may receive the reward of His suffering!**

I'm sure you will agree that this is something higher than compassion for the lost, this is the difference between a God-centred vision and a man-centred vision. There is a place for tears. There is a place for a burden for the lost. There is a place to be moved by physical suffering. But these motivations are enriched when they are the fruit of a greater vision: a vision of God's glory. This is the end-game. This is what it's all headed towards. "… ministering as a priest the gospel of God, so that my offering of the Gentiles may become acceptable …" (Rom. 15:16)

After this I looked and saw a multitude too large to count, from every nation and tribe and people and tongue, standing before the throne and before the Lamb. They were wearing white robes and holding palm branches in their hands. And they cried out in a loud voice:

> "Salvation to our God,
> who sits on the throne,
> and to the Lamb!"

(Rev 7:9-10)

John Piper captures the essential essence of this principle, in his book, 'Let the Nations Be Glad'.

> Worship, therefore, is the fuel and goal of missions. It's the goal of missions because in missions we simply aim to bring the nations into the white hot enjoyment of God's glory. The goal of missions is the gladness of the peoples in the greatness of God. "The Lord reigns; let the earth rejoice; let the many coastlands be glad!" (Ps 97:1). "Let the peoples praise thee, O God; let all the peoples praise thee! Let the nations be glad and sing for joy!" (Ps 67:3-4).
>
> But worship is also the fuel of missions. Passion for God in worship precedes the offer of God in preaching. You can't commend what you don't cherish. Missionaries will never call out, "Let the nations be glad!" who cannot say from the heart, "I rejoice in the Lord...I will be glad and exult in thee, I will sing praise to thy name, O Most High" (Ps 104:34, 9:2). Missions begins and ends in worship."

Compassion for the lost is needed, but we must continually re-baptise our compassion for the lost in the sea of God's glory. Only a God-centred vision will keep the fire burning. Only a God-centred vision will deliver us from fleshly religious performance. A vision of the glory of God will fuel our passion and it will transform our vision.

When you walk through your streets, in your town, or in your city, what do you see? Yes – see the lost, see the needs, and see the brokenness – but look beyond the ground level chaos and peer into the spiritual heavens that radiate with the splendour and glory of God. Don't just preach the gospel so that sinners can be saved from hell, or so the emotionally broken can be made whole – preach the gospel with such heaven-birthed glory radiating from your eyes, face and words that the very atmosphere becomes charged with a sense of God's glory. God himself is the good news. The end-goal is not the benefits of the gospel, the end-goal is the very source of the gospel: God himself.

When I first became a Christian, a lot of the preachers I saw out on the streets looked absolutely miserable. Prophets of doom who looked like they were carrying the world on their shoulders. And I imagine they were. They were probably carrying the weight of lost people. Sadly, they only had half the story. Their fuel was the fear of hell. They did not know about the joy of God's glory. Or if they did, they certainly didn't manifest it.

Thankfully things are changing. There is a new generation of street preachers, many of them young folk, who have encountered something of God's glory. They don't just take a message to the streets, they take his presence to the streets. They are not just preachers, they are worshippers and they take worship to the streets. As they worship in spirit and in truth, the atmosphere is transformed. Yes they preach the cross, they preach the judgement to come, they preach repentance but they charge the atmosphere with spiritual glory and authority.

I didn't understand these principles in the early

days when I first went out to the streets. As a result, the teams I went out with were often affected by the spiritual atmosphere around them. The darkness was dominant. However, when you carry a spirit of worship, and you take that to the streets, you step into authority. The anointing and the presence of God manifests through God's people and the atmosphere is filled with light and life and freedom. There are times you can almost see the darkness lift. "The light shines in the darkness, and the darkness can never extinguish it." (John 1:5)

How can we make sure our motivation is right? We need to visit the throne room. As we align our hearts with the God of glory, the God of love, and the God of all power and authority, our hearts will be transformed by his presence. He is a King, we are his ambassadors, and where we go – the King goes. Let's lay hold of the gospel of the Kingdom, and the King who commissions us. Consequently, we won't be intimidated by the darkness, the darkness will be intimidated by us. We can move forward in mission with confidence because our vision isn't limited by present circumstances, instead our hearts are burning with a glorious vision of the Kingdom which has come, is coming and one day will come in all its glorious fullness.

CHAPTER FOUR: STREETS RIPE FOR HARVEST: CATCHING THE VISION OF JESUS

Don't you have a saying, 'It's still four months until harvest'? I tell you, open your eyes and look at the fields! They are ripe for harvest. (John 4:35)

"Look on the world with the eyes of Jesus. There are people and peoples reaching harvest time all around us and all around the world. Don't be fatalistic or mechanistic. Lift up your eyes and see that God is readying harvest all the time." (John Piper)

Jesus could see things his disciples could not, and it wasn't because of divine omniscience, it was due to his spiritual vision. Jesus knew his identity, and his purpose and calling. His eye was always on the Father's work. His heart was in tune with his Father's mission, and that sensitivity enabled him to see people and circumstances through a different lens not that which everyone else looked through.

In this passage in John chapter four, we are given a glimpse into Jesus' 'street ministry' and evangelism. We see that his disciples are blinkered and distracted by mundane things like grabbing lunch, or social politics – Jesus shouldn't be speaking to a woman (and certainly not a Samaritan woman) yet Jesus shows that he was willing to step beyond social norms, and break through barrios of prejudice in order to reach a person with the life-giving gospel. Jesus saw the divine appointment in this meeting with the woman of Samaria, but he could also see that she would be instrumental in reaching her own community. He sowed a seed and expected a harvest.

Let's look at a section of this encounter. Jesus engages the woman in conversation, and helps lift her eyes from natural things (water) to spiritual things (living water) and he draws her mind from shallow sectarian issues to the meaning of true worship. He then draws her into a revelation of himself. This revelation leads to a conviction of sin, and a glimpse of the grace of God that is offered in Christ. Just at this point of climax, the disciples come back. They should have been in awe at what they were seeing. They should have been buzzing because a woman was in the process of encountering Christ and his grace. But they didn't have eyes to see.

> Just then his disciples returned and were surprised to find him talking with a woman. But no one asked, "What do you want?" or "Why are you talking with her?"
>
> Then, leaving her water jar, the woman went back to the town and said to the people, "Come, see a man who told me everything I ever did. Could this be the Messiah?" They came out of the town and made their way toward him.
>
> Meanwhile his disciples urged him, "Rabbi, eat

something."

But he said to them, "I have food to eat that you know nothing about."

Then his disciples said to each other, "Could someone have brought him food?"

"My food," said Jesus, "is to do the will of him who sent me and to finish his work. Don't you have a saying, 'It's still four months until harvest'? I tell you, open your eyes and look at the fields! They are ripe for harvest. Even now the one who reaps draws a wage and harvests a crop for eternal life, so that the sower and the reaper may be glad together. Thus the saying 'One sows and another reaps' is true. I sent you to reap what you have not worked for. Others have done the hard work, and you have reaped the benefits of their labor." (John 4:27-38)

This narrative gives us a keen insight into the contrast between the attitude of Jesus and the attitude of the disciples. The disciples are caught up in their criticism of their leader, although they aren't confident enough to challenge him directly – nonetheless their internal criticisms are predominant in their minds. Then after she leaves, they start to tell him what he should be doing – "here Jesus, you need to eat something!" I'm sure they were well meaning, but they were also misguided. But before we judge them, stop for a minute. Are we any different? How much time is consumed in church life by people unhappy at how the pastor or leaders are doing things? How many times do well-meaning (but misguided) people approach their leader to tell them what they need to be doing? The disciples were suffering from valley vision. Their perspective was limited to the lowlands of this life. And the truth is, 21st century Christians are no different. In fact we are probably worse. We are so caught up in carnal, fleshly, and soulish thinking that we don't realise just how much within us needs to be dealt with if we hope to become more aligned with the missional heart of God.

Carnal people will object here: "Doesn't God want us to eat?" Of course he does, that's not the point. The point is, the desires of the disciples' bellies and their judgemental outlook was clashing with the missional moment. That can happen to us too, the judgements which spring from our unrenewed mind, and our basic human desires and disposition towards looking out for our primary needs, all cloud our vision. We no longer see the vision of Christ, or feel his heart-beat. All we hear and feel is our groaning bellies.

So Jesus challenges them,

"I tell you, open your eyes and look at the fields! They are ripe for harvest."

We need to be challenged too.

Open your eyes and look to the streets! They are ripe for harvest!"

In other words, there are individuals, every day, walking through our streets, waiting for their divine appointment. Some may not know it. Some may be searching. Others may be running away from it, but it's there. All you and I need to do is follow the example of Jesus. Break out of the comfort zone, follow the leading of the Spirit, go to the city well (the places where people gather) and look for an opportunity to engage. Once the opportunity comes, make an invitation. Invite people to encounter and taste the living water of Christ's presence.

Never under-estimate the potential of an individual divine appointment. If you reach one person, you have no idea how many people that one person will reach.

> Many of the Samaritans from that town believed in him because of the woman's testimony, "He told me everything I ever did." So when the Samaritans came to him, they urged him to stay with them, and he stayed two days. And because of his words many more became believers.
>
> They said to the woman, "We no longer believe just because of what you said; now we have heard for ourselves, and we know that this man really is the Savior of the world." (John 4:39-42)

This is the harvest that Jesus envisioned.

Jesus desired that his disciples would see the lost through his eyes. He wanted them to catch his vision, and his heart for the harvest. Don't get me wrong, a vision of the harvest is not a guarantee of immediate results. Jesus makes this point clear. He says: "'One sows and another reaps' is true. I sent you to reap what you have not worked for. Others have done the hard work, and you have reaped the benefits of their labor." Sometimes we get to sow, sometimes we get to reap, and other times we get the really hard work of ploughing up a stony field. Only the vision of a harvest will sustain us. It's not about reaping the results, it's about faithfulness to the vision. However, if we don't see, we won't sow and if we don't sow we will never see a harvest.

Imagine what could happen if every local church began to be gripped by a vision of the harvest? Imagine what could happen if we started to see our streets through the eyes of Christ. What if we went out to the streets, in teams, with gospel-intentionality? What if we went out to the streets with expectation? Think about it – God is sovereign, he can empty the streets of everyone he doesn't want there, and fill the streets with everyone he does want there. We are called to partner with God. What if God honoured your obedience by filling the streets with people who are ready to receive Christ? Impossible? Not with God it's not!

It's my conviction that the streets *are* ripe for harvest! There are people ready to receive Christ. There are people ready to hear. The only thing missing is the preacher. If your church is like many churches, you already have an army of missionaries. Why not take your prayer-ministry team, your prayer-warriors, your praise and worship leaders and your preachers out to the streets? Why don't you kick off some praise and worship in the city centre? Why not take some of that bold, exuberant and passionate worship that you experience in church and let it loose on the streets? I can guarantee you this – if you do – power will be released. Release your ministry teams to pray for people in the streets. How do you do that? The same way you do in a service – invite people to come forward for prayer. And those testimonies you have in your church? Give those people a microphone and tell them they have two minutes to share how Jesus changed their life. And preacher – stir that passion and proclaim Christ in the streets with every fibre of your being. Preach as a dying man (or woman!) to dying people. And don't just preach – call people to repentance. Invite people to respond. And while you are at it, why not set up some large paddling pools and baptise people on the streets. Why not? John the Baptist did it publicly, Jesus and his disciples did it publicly, and the apostles did it publicly. The harvest is plentiful, but the labourers are few – it's time to see the harvest and it's time to gather in the harvest. All you need is a willing heart and confidence in the blood of Jesus Christ and the power of the Holy Spirit. As you proclaim Christ in the streets, heaven will flood the atmosphere. That's not wishful thinking. That is simply what Jesus promised. It's why the Holy Spirit was given! What are you waiting for? The harvest awaits!

CHAPTER FIVE: TAKING THE KINGDOM TO THE STREETS

Jesus went throughout Galilee, teaching in their synagogues, proclaiming the good news of the kingdom, and healing every disease and sickness among the people. (Matt 4:23)

"The kingdom is about doing just as much as teaching. If you aren't doing the works of the kingdom the message isn't complete." John Wimber

Streets have different connotations for different people. City streets during the day at the height of summer give a different vibe to the same city streets after dark. City streets can be places of life, activity and culture. And they can be a place of vice, crime and violence. Often the two vibes run in parallel. Writing this book in 2022 is strange because one of the things that has happened during the Covid pandemic is that our streets and public squares were, for a time, no-go areas. The streets, for a time, were deserted. But people are returning to the streets. Just last summer (2021) I had the joy of leading *Hope on the Streets*, a city centre open air, in partnership with other local churches and an evangelistic ministry which came up from England. We held these events on the streets of Stirling in Scotland. On both occasions, despite recent lockdowns, the streets were bustling and people were open to engaging with us.

I've been involved with various forms of street ministry for over twenty years. I've handed out gospel tracts on the streets, led small preaching teams and preached the gospel in various towns all over Scotland (Paisley; Johnstone, Greenock, Glasgow, Largs, Dunblane, Stornoway in Lewis, Portree (Skye), Perth and Stirling amongst other places); I've spoken at large inter-church Open Air Events; led detached youth work teams in some of the most deprived schemes in Renfrewshire and I've led prayer events in public places – which almost every time result in a powerful missional encounter. I've encountered setbacks and successes, demonstrations of God's power and times of discouragement. There have been times when it has seemed as if nothing happened, and there have been times that felt as if revival was about to break out. Street ministry is like the seasons, there is a variety of contrasting experiences that accompany it. Most of the time street ministry is a joy. There is no greater joy that I know than the joy of testifying of Christ in the frontlines and seeing the Kingdom of God at work.

One of the aspects I'm keen to stress at this point is this: *we are not just called to proclaim the gospel in the streets, we are called to take the kingdom of God to the streets.* This is important. The streets need to not only hear about the Kingdom, they need to see the Kingdom. As a church we can take mercy ministry to the streets when we go out and feed people on the streets. When we do this we are showing forth the Kingdom of God and creating a space for people to hear about the Kingdom and to receive the Kingdom. One of the biggest tragedies in the church is the fact that social action and evangelism have been separated. The evangelicals have run with evangelism and have become suspicious about social action, and the social gospel people have run with social and action but have become suspicious of evangelism. The two were never supposed to be separated, they are both part and parcel of the Kingdom of God. Jesus used words *and* deeds, and so should we.

We are also called to go to the streets in the power of the Spirit. Prayer groups, and healing ministry is for the streets. One of the reasons why we don't see more healing manifest in the church is because healing is a sign that is intended to follow the proclamation of the gospel. Want to see more signs? Go with the gospel to the darkest places in your city and you will see God's supernatural power at work. That's the reason he supplies us with His Spirit in the first place – it is to empower our mission. Signs point to the reality. The gifts of the Spirit are not given so churches can have a great Holy Spirit time to themselves, the gifts of the Spirit are ultimately given to equip us and empower us for mission.

I once was part of a Pentecostal church in a small deprived community. The church was small and struggling and soon merged with another Pentecostal church that seemed to be thriving. The new church had exciting praise, all the cool new songs, a skilled and anointed praise band. The church also had good Bible teaching. However, the church (at that time) had very little connection with the surrounding community. To me it seemed as if everyone was driving into this run down area in their nice cars, stepping over the poverty on their way in to church, and stepping back over it again on their way out, as they returned to their nice cars, in their nice clothes to drive back to their nice houses for their nice lunches. I said this to one of the members at the time. It didn't go down well.

Sometime later, the Lord created an opportunity. I'd taken up a post as a detached youth worker in the area. My job was to work along-side a team of youth workers, engage the young people who were hanging around the streets, and help guide them towards more positive life choices. There had been a series of violent incidents – buses were set on fire, gangs were fighting, a young person had been shot outside the snooker hall – it was mental. Our project had street workers and financial resources, but there was a problem, our project was only funded for two years. This is when I knew we needed to partner with the local church.

Between the youth project and the church, we began to see some real community work blossom. In addition to the street work, we worked with the church to set up a new youth project. Sessional staff were employed. We paid for the local five-aside football pitches so that the young folk could access them and play some football. We were able to bring in a council sports worker who provided training under his remit as community worker. And it just so happened he was a Christian (another sign of the Kingdom at work). For me, one of the highlights was when a group of young people from the church got involved. They went out to the local MUGA (Multi-Use Games Arena) which was full of litter, and covered with shards of broken glass (it had just become a drinking area) and they swept it clean. They made it fit for purpose again. They young team saw this and it had an effect. It didn't matter that it would soon fall into disrepair again. The young folk from the church sent out a missional message to the young folk from the scheme: *you matter, we care, and God cares*. That church project continued long after our funding dried up and we'd moved on, but it was great example of the Kingdom of God being manifest through the church on the streets.

Some of the greatest encounters I've experienced on the streets have not been when we have set out to preach, but rather when we have set out to engage in Kingdom works. A number of years ago, myself and a friend started a prayer event in George Square. The purpose was not evangelism, the purpose was to call local Christians to public prayer, repentance and intercession. Those were great prayer meetings, and one of the unintentional outcomes of those meetings was the fact that evangelism happened spontaneously. When we take the Kingdom to the market place, we shouldn't be surprised when the Holy Spirit creates some divine appointments.

CHAPTER SIX: STREET ENCOUNTERS

"The Holy Spirit said to Philip, "Go over and walk along beside the carriage."" Acts 8:29

"To be a soul winner is the happiest thing in the world. And with every soul you bring to Jesus Christ, you seem to get a new heaven here upon earth." Charles Spurgeon

One of the most thrilling parts of street ministry is the sense you get that there has been a divine appointment. I'm not just talking about when someone comes to the Lord. I'm talking about encounters with individuals or groups that result in something significant happening. In recent years, I've found there is usually at least one divine appointment every time I'm involved in some form of street ministry. I've also found that missional opportunities present themselves even when we were not setting out to look for them. On example of this was a prayer walk that I organised for our church plant. As we headed out to the streets of Stirling, we bumped into a young couple who I'd happened to meet on the Teen Challenge bus the night before. One of our church members also serves on the Teen Challenge bus, and she knew the couple well. After a brief conversation, the guy asked for prayer – so we laid hands on the couple and prayed for them. It's my conviction that praying for people, with the laying on of hands, is a key way for people to encounter the presence of God. So we prayed. After this the guy asked for my number. Later that night I received a message from him on *Whats App*: "Thanks for that touching prayer John, I got mad tingles/ energy through my body, hopefully a new lease of life, thank you."

What did he experience? What was it he felt? (One cynical Teen Challenge worker quipped: "It was just the drugs." I'm more prone to believe it was the presence of God. When you are on drugs, you are already aware of the buzz that you have. He was indicating that he felt something different. The Holy Spirit has the power to break through any haze of substances and make his presence known.

If street ministry is a new concept for you or your church, I'd encourage you and your church to begin with prayer walking. Over the years I've heard conservative evangelicals mock the idea of prayer walks: "God is sovereign, he doesn't need to be where you are praying. He is already there." What is overlooked is this: prayer walking is not about what God is able to do, it's about what God is able to do *in you* when you put yourself in the mission field. Walking the location doesn't change anything in God, but sure changes us. God can begin to open our eyes to see what he wants us to see. He can bring people across our paths. These opportunities are missed when we lock ourselves away to pray in our church buildings.

I believe there is a principle, if we will walk the

streets and pray over our cities asking God to save the lost, he will give us opportunities. This is exactly what happened when a friend and I pioneered weekly public prayer events (Prayer for the Land) in George Square, Glasgow. Here are some extracts of testimonies that I published on a website at the time.

John's Account

Prayer for the Land was really a response from two Christian friends to this example in the life of E.M Bounds.

> Bounds took over as pastor of Franklin's Methodist Episcopal Church. Of course, he had his usual duties as a pastor, his usual responsibilities to his congregation, but his eye was on the larger picture. He entreated God to show him a way to lift the sorrow and darkness that engulfed the entire town. Then one day God answered his prayer with an idea. Bounds would call the men of the town to join him in prayer every Tuesday evening in the town square and cry out to God for their city. Even if the idea might have seemed farfetched and frankly much too simplistic to work, the men gave it a try. For months, every Tuesday evening, they would gather on their knees in the town square and pray that the sorrow and darkness would lift. Slowly, surely it worked.
>
> For over a year the faithful band called upon the Lord until God finally answered by fire. The revival came down without any previous announcement or plan, and without the pastor sending for an evangelist to help him. Not only did Franklin Tennessee, begin to heal, but God began to touch hearts and awaken spirits all over town. Bound's own congre-

gation exploded from a few faithful believers to five hundred...Bounds said "Revivals are among the charter rights of the church. A revival means a broken-hearted pastor. A revival means a church on its knees confessing its sins- the sins of the individual and of the church - confessing the sins of the times and of the community".

Taken from E.M Bounds *The Classic Collection On Prayer* page xvii

As I read of this account something in my spirit was stirred. I thought to myself - imagine a group of Christians gathering in George Square every week to cry out to God in repentance and faith for a move of God in our own city and nation. What a sight this would be.

I later read this section of the book to my friend and concluded with the question 'can you imagine this every week in George Square?' This met with an immediate 'I'm up for that!' We took it to the Lord in prayer and the Holy Spirit seemed to confirm that this was indeed from Him by the sense of His presence that began to touch our hearts. We decided to head down to George Square that night to commit it to the Lord in prayer.

As we prayed in the Square that Saturday night, it was somewhere between 10-11pm, and we could not but help become aware of the chaos that filled the streets. We prayed for about half an hour or so and as we were finishing up we were approached by a young man who wanted to know what we were doing. He had been drinking, and he shared openly about many of the difficulties he found himself in. We listened, identified, shared something of our testimonies with him as well as explaining something of the gospel. He allowed us to pray for him and he took a Bible from us. As we parted company we felt something of the Lord's confirmation that this was right. We felt that a divine appointment had taken place and our eyes were opened afresh to 1) the great needs of those who do not know Christ and 2) our own weakness and helplessness and 3) the need for God to move in power through His Spirit and His word.

The following Sunday we notified our churches and leaders of our plans to meet weekly in George Square for prayer. Permission was granted to share the vision with others in our churches in order to generate interest. In this sense Prayer for the Land is a gathering of Christians from local churches but is not a ministry of the local church that either of us attend.

Prayer for the Land starts Monday 17th August

If your spirit was moved by the account of E.M Bounds call to prayer and if you have a burden to see Christ glorified in the land of Scotland. If you are convinced that the only answer for our nation's problems is the gospel. Then feel free to join us in calling upon the name of the Lord for our city and our nation every Monday 8-9pm at George Square beginning Mon 17th August.

David's Account of the First Night

When John and I prayed in George Square just over a week ago we attracted the attention of a young man who was sitting drinking on one of the benches. So when there are a dozen of us praying it is not surprising that we also attract attention. When one of our number had just finished praying, a young Goth burst into the centre of our circle and announced that he was an agnostic and demanded proof of God. His two friends stayed on the outside of the circle and the man who had just finished praying offered to go and speak with him on the outside of the circle. Although the prayer meeting continued our numbers were depleted as some of our number left the circle to witness to the other young people who were demanding answers from us. Every one of us was encouraged, first of all by the opposition that we received but also from the end result that saw a group of young people hearing about the God of love from people whose Christianity is of a vibrant nature.

I have been to many prayer meetings as a Christian and sadly many of them were uneventful and left nothing that I would remember them by - the memory of this prayer meeting will be with me for the rest of my life and I really believe that this is only the beginning - I await the next one with eager anticipation and honestly can't wait till it's Monday again.

We have a great God, a loving Father, a God who is slow to anger and who abounds in love. It is an absolute blessing being able to stand in a public place and raise up His name and the name of His Son, Jesus. If you have nothing doing on Monday nights, why not join us?

Another account from John

Last night at PFTL there was a real sense of an open heaven. As I pulled up the car at George Square and paused for a moment to quieten my heart before the Lord I sensed the presence of the Lord flow over me and through me like liquid love. A prophetess from the States turned up at the meeting and encouraged our hearts in the Lord. She carried a burden for the nations, and an anticipation for revival in Scotland. As she prayed I sensed an inner strengthening and something of God's glory touch the meeting. As God's presence fell there was a liberty that began to rise up in the spirit realm. At this point some of the young people and other passers-by began to approach the prayer meeting and spontaneous evangelism broke out once again. I believe as we continue to press in we shall see more and more of this sort of thing taking place.

Someone once said. "When I pray, coincidences

happen, when I don't pray, they stop." There is a similar principle with divine appointments on the street. When I go to the streets, whether it be to pray or to preach, divine appointments happen, when I don't – they don't.

CHAPTER SEVEN: SOWING AND REAPING

'The saying 'One sows and another reaps' is true. I sent you to reap what you have not worked for. Others have done the hard work, and you have reaped the benefits of their labor.' (John 4:37)

"Evangelism is like a sower scattering seed–some of it falls on bad soil and brings forth very little fruit, and some of it falls on good soil and brings forth a great deal of fruit. Jesus explained that the seed is like the Word of God." Billy Graham

"Does preaching in the street work?" This is a question I encountered a lot during the early days of my street ministry. It wasn't really a question. It was really a rhetorical question. The question was usually delivered in a disdainful tone, from a professional Christian with an upturned nose and a posh accent. The question reveals more issues with the person asking it, than it does the effectiveness of a particular evangelistic method. If I'd known this classic D.L. Moody quote in the early days, I'd have simply responded with this brilliant illustration:

> One day a lady criticized D.L. Moody for his methods of evangelism in attempting to win people to the Lord. Moody's reply was "I agree with you. I don't like the way I do it either. Tell me, how do you do it?" The lady re-

plied, "I don't do it." Moody responded, "I like my way of doing it better than your way of not doing it."

The idea that street evangelism "doesn't work" exposes a fatal flaw in our understanding of what Jesus has called us to do. Jesus did not say: "Go and preach the gospel to all creation – *if* it works." He simply called us to deliver the mail. It's up to individuals to choose what they do with the message. Our job is simply to be faithful messengers. We sow the seed, we water the seed, but only God can give growth. "So then neither he who plants is anything, nor he who waters, but God who gives the increase." (1 Cor 3:7)

Only God can produce results in a person's heart. Judging evangelism by immediate results or apparent success is a symptom of pragmatism. It's a bit like telling a farmer he's wasting his time sowing seed in the ground because there is no obvious or immediate sign of growth.

There are times when the Lord when the Lord lets us see the joys of our labour, and there are times when we see no results. There are also times when we reap the results of other people's labours. Just because a person comes to Christ under your ministry does not mean that *your* methods are better than anyone else's For all you know you are reaping the results of decades of prayers. Maybe this person has had seeds sown from various people. At the end of the day, salvation is from the Lord, not you or me. We are simply called to sow the seed.

I recall a time (sometime around 2002) when our

church was under a severe spiritual attack. I was on the bus, on my way to Bible College, when a righteous indignation rose up within me. I felt this indignation rise up – "How dare the enemy seek to intimidate us, and get us off track." I felt an urge to preach the gospel in the centre of Glasgow. On my way back from the Bible College, I found my spot, whipped out my New Testament (I carried with me everywhere in those days) and began to preach from the verse: "I am the light of the world. Whoever follows me will not walk in darkness, but will have the light of life." (John 8:12) A few minutes into my message, a couple of teenage guys (about 13 years old) stopped and watched me with a bemused look. "What are you doing?" One of them asked.

"I'm trying to help people understand that there is a God, and that they can know him."

"But no one is listening," replied one of them – looking around at all the folk walking by.

"*I'm* listening." Replied his mate, without missing a beat.

That to me was a priceless moment. It taught me a lesson. I was about to agree with the first wee guy, that no one was listening. But the second lad taught me something. Even when it seems that no one is listening, people *are* listening. *Someone* is listening. I was encouraged at his mate's confidence in being able to be upfront about the fact that he was taking something of the message in. The moral of the story? Just because people are walking by the street preacher, doesn't mean they aren't hearing something. Over the years I've come to believe that God uses sound bites for various individuals as they walk past the preaching of the gospel. Little truth bombs that land where they are supposed to. We need to remember that there is power in the Word of God.

Let's talk about results for moment. Over the many years I've been preaching in the streets, it's never led to new people joining *my* church. I know other street evangelists have had more success in this area. But I've not. However, there are around four individuals that I later found out did make professions of faith, and did get plugged into local churches. I recall meeting a guy in a new church plant in Paisley. I knew he seemed familiar. He was a guy my street team had met one day we were preaching in the streets. He'd been sitting in a doorway, lost and with no hope. Another guy was drinking in a waste ground area in Ferguslie Park. I was walking my dog, I gave him a tract and spoke briefly with him about Jesus. I heard some months later that he had joined the local Church of Scotland and had cleaned himself up. Another time I was playing my guitar and singing in the street and a woman came up to me. She was bound in alcohol addiction. She and her husband had gone to Las Vegas and had tried their hand at the casinos. They lost all their money and caught a gambling addiction. She had lost everything. Now she was on the streets begging me to give her money. I spoke with her about Jesus. Months later I met her in a local Baptist church, she was with May Nicholson, a powerful woman of God who was used mightily to help people who were caught in addiction. This woman was attending May's meetings and on the road to recovery. Another time I met a guy with huge mental health issues. He was deeply distressed and oppressed by demonic powers. Again, after sharing the gospel with him, he ended up in church, his life changed, and he even became a preacher himself.

Am I saying that it was *my* ministry that led these folk to the Lord? No. But I am saying that I believe those street encounters were part of several links in the chain that ultimately led each of these individuals to begin to follow Jesus and connect with a local church. When we take the gospel to the streets, we are simply doing our part. It's a kingdom endeavour. It's not about getting bums on seats in *our* church. It's about serving the kingdom.

CHAPTER EIGHT: STREET MINISTRY IS TEAM MINISTRY

"Calling the Twelve to him, he began to send them out two by two." (Mark 6:7)

"After this, the Lord chose 72 more followers. He sent them out in groups of two." (Luke 10:1)

"The kingdom is about doing just as much as teaching. If you aren't doing the works of the kingdom the message isn't complete. I pray the Vineyard never stops taking the risks of the kingdom." John Wimber

Street ministry is team ministry. This is an essential principle. Street ministry, if it is to be truly effective, must be a church ministry. Street ministry is not an individual ministry (although God can use individuals powerfully in the streets.) The best street projects are street projects that release multiple ministries into the streets.

Not everyone is gifted at preaching. Not everyone is an evangelist. However, there are people in your church who are prayer warriors. They have a role to pray. They can be part of the street team who quietly stand whilst the event is happening, and they can be praying. There are people in your church with a healing ministry. They can be there to pray for anyone who is suffering and in pain and who would like prayer. There will be people with a prophetic gifting in your church. These are folk who are able to bring a word in season into people's lives. They have a role to play in street events. Worship leaders can lead worship. Is there a hospitality team? Why not have them serve free hot drinks on the streets whilst others hand out tracts and preach the gospel? When we mobilise the whole body of Christ for street ministry, we allow more of Jesus to be seen on the streets. The diverse gifts within God's people are given to reveal Jesus. The bigger, and more diverse the street team, the more of Jesus is revealed in the streets.

Whilst not every Christian is an evangelist, I am of the view that every Christian should be able to share their testimony with unbelievers, and they should also, at least once, give their testimony in the open air. It's only fear that holds people back from doing that. The apostle Peter says that every believer should be ready and willing to give the reason for the hope that they have. Well, what better place to do this than in the open air?

> But in your hearts revere Christ as Lord. Always be prepared to give an answer to everyone who asks you to give the reason for the hope that you have. But do this with gentleness and respect. (1 Peter 3:15)

Not every Christian is an evangelist, but evangelists are given to equip the church for works of ministry (Ephesians 4). This ministry includes ministry to the lost. It includes taking the gospel to those who are outside of Christ. God anoints individuals, but mission has to ultimately be a collective enterprise. At the very least, every local church should look for opportunities to take what they do inside a church building out to the public places. When weather allows we should be having church in the streets, church in the park, and church in the square.

There is a reason Jesus sent out his disciples in

teams.

Firstly, mission is risky. It's not unusual to encounter opposition and there is safety in numbers. Occasionally (as I've shown already) I have preached on my own. I know other experienced evangelists have done this too. I'm used to the risks that can be encountered on the streets. I had a number of dangerous street encounters before I was a Christian. In one sense my pre-Christian street experience still shapes me today. I can handle most situations. That said, we need to be wise. As a principle, we shouldn't go alone. Occasionally the Spirit may lead us to spontaneously do something in the streets on our own, but ideally we should build a team and do ministry as a team.

Secondly, as I hinted at earlier, the more diverse the team, the more varied the street ministry is, the more people from your church can play a part. Include everyone. If there are tables, signs, and equipment to be set up, recruit the set up team. They can also be there as part of the crowd. A crowd attracts a crowd. One of the things that will happen is folk will begin to move from practical ministry to speaking to people about their faith. If you are just there to set up equipment, there is every chance someone from the street will talk to you and ask what you are doing. For me, I started serving tea on a Teen Challenge bus in a drug riddled community. I wasn't there to share my faith – but it began to happen naturally. Clients began to ask me why I was on the bus – it was a chance to share my story. It happened without even trying. The streets are no different.

The principle of a strong team was not something I appreciated when I first started doing street ministry. I'd either be out alone, or with a couple of other guys. All of us zealous and intense evangelists. It was only in 2010 that I really came to see the value and importance of recruiting a stronger team. I approached my pastor about doing some open air work in Portree square. The pastor was supportive, but he said one thing: "get a team." This was wisdom. I recruited a team. In the end we had about a dozen folks. Some were there to hand out tracts, others were there to pray quietly, some were there to share testimony (2 minutes each), some were there to sing gospel songs and others were there to preach a short gospel message. It was one of the most positive, light-hearted and vibrant street events I'd experienced up until that point. If your street team is limited to a couple of strong guys, folks on the street may find you intimidating. If you are part of diverse group of men, women, children and folks of all ages, smiling and having a good time, the whole thing is less threatening and much more inviting. Street ministry is team ministry because it's ultimately a ministry of the body of Christ.

Thirdly, the bigger and stronger the team, the more opportunity there is to expand the street ministry. What are the needs in your local community? Is there a lack of sports provision? Could your street ministry coordinate football for the local young team in the park? Does your church have decent resources? Why not set up a pop-up five-aside football pitch in an appropriate area? The opportunities are endless. As churches we can hand out food hampers, advent calendars, Easter eggs, hot-drinks, or we can give away free burgers, hotdogs and drinks if the weather is good. We can set up bouncy castles and fun activities at local parks. The opportunities are endless, and the streets are ripe for harvest. Individuals can't do everything, but together as a team, we can take the light and love of Jesus to our streets and public places.

Finally, the reason street ministry needs to be a team ministry is because it's more biblical. The idea of *the* man of God or God's man of power for the hour is part of our evangelical and Pentecostal folklore but these historical giants didn't function in isolation, they all had a team. Even our Lord and saviour Jesus Christ (and if anyone could have flown solo, he could have!) didn't try to fulfil his ministry without a team. The first thing he did was call 12 team members. He then built the team to over 70. By the time he ascended to glory, there were 120 (plus women and children) waiting in an upper room, and on the verge of being launched by the Spirit out into new spheres of ministry.

CHAPTER NINE: ANOINTING: THE SOURCE OF IMPACT AND AUTHORITY

The Spirit of the Lord is upon me, because he has anointed me to proclaim good news to the poor. He has sent me to proclaim liberty to the captives and recovering of sight to the blind, to set at liberty those who are oppressed. (Luke 4:18)

"We function as full members of God's anointed, prophetic, interceding, healing community only because of what Jesus did at Calvary and at Pentecost. We experience forgiveness from sin and victory over sin because of the atoning cross, and we receive power to live and to witness through the Pentecostal anointing." Colin Dye

The greatest need for any Christian ministry is the anointing of the Holy Spirit. The anointing is God's empowering presence, resting upon us, working through us, and enlivening and enriching our work for the Lord. The anointing imparts life into the message and the messenger. Despite our need for the anointing, so many aspects of ministry function without the anointing. We have unanointed sermons, unanointed worship, and unanointed church programmes. There are many reasons for this. Too many to go into in this chapter. We even have unanointed street preaching. Un-anointed street preaching has possibly done more damage to the cause of street ministry than any other issue. Unanointed street preaching carries a spirit of death (just like unanointed pulpit ministry). I've encountered several examples of unanointed street preaching, and you probably have too. Sadly, very few of us have encountered anointed street preaching. That's because there isn't much of it around. But it does happen, and I'm encouraged by the signs that seem to indicate that God is raising up a new generation of street evangelists. These evangelists are often young, edgy, and have been saved from the depths of sin. They've tasted hell, and they have been rescued by God's amazing grace, and they have been sent into the harvest field to rescue others. When a man or a woman has been to hell and back, their message carries a ring of authenticity. They don't stand preaching like a Pharisee to tax collectors, they kneel, imploring people to receive Christ's mercy, grace and healing.

Having said this, not every professing believer is able to recognise the true anointing. Some Christians assume if a message is strong, hard-hitting, and challenging that it isn't anointed. That's just not the case, in fact, it's because the gospel is strong, hard-hitting, and challenging that we need the anointing! At its heart the gospel is a call to repent of sin. If you are going to preach to a sin celebrating crowd, you better make sure you have the anointing.

The anointing will give your message authority. And people – even lost people – recognise authority.

Matthew writes: "When Jesus had finished saying these things, the crowds were amazed at his teaching, because he taught as one who had authority, and not as their teachers of the law." (Matt 7:28-29) This is the effect of the anointing. The religious leaders did not carry the anointing because their religious attitudes disqualified them from walking in the anointing. The key to the anointing is Christ, and religion rejects Christ, and instead operates out of the flesh. As I've said before, religious people will head out to the streets, but they carry a message of death.

I once lived in a small village in Renfrewshire. There was a small gospel hall in the village, and it was the only evangelical church in the area. The group were extremely traditionalist, prone to legalism, and totally elitist. They considered themselves to be the only true church, and every other church was in error. They also did street preaching.

However, the street preaching involved heading out from the church and walking to a street that was full of flats, and pointing a handheld amplifier towards a certain flat, and releasing a barrage of strong statements about hellfire and judgement for people who turn away from God. I later discovered an ex-member of their church lived in that flat, and that is why they were doing it. A ministry of death.

One other example is when I was scheduled to meet up with a street evangelism team in Paisley. I hadn't met them before. I walked down the high street and saw two preachers with signs and assumed it was them. Only upon approaching them did I realise my mistake. As they began to speak to me, my eye caught the writings on some of their signs: "Babbling in tongues is witchcraft"; "Churches laughing in the Spirit are possessed by demons!"

These guys were hard-core cessationists, (people who think the gifts of the Holy Spirit have passed away) unattached to a local church, and they were bringing an embittered in-house church debate into the streets. That kind of thing just spreads confusion and is an embarrassment to the church. The same can be said for those who confuse preaching the gospel with political issues or even the preaching of moralism. The gospel speaks to our morals, but there is a difference between standing in the streets and preaching a moral code, and preaching Christ. One message is centred in religion, the other is grounded in the grace of God.

We are not called to take a list of rules out to the street, we are called to provide water to the thirsty, bread for the hungry, and healing for the broken. This is what brings the anointing. The anointing is like a shaft of light into the darkness.

I mentioned earlier that the anointing enables you to walk in spiritual authority. You need this for street ministry. If you are taking the gospel to the streets, you are walking into the devil's territory. There will be spiritual opposition. Sometimes that opposition will be thick in the air. At other times it will manifest through the people. You need to walk in authority, otherwise you will be oppressed and intimidated by the atmosphere. When you walk in the authority of the anointing, you will find the surrounding darkness subject to you, not you intimidated by the darkness. There have been times when I've been out in the streets and there has just been a wonderful sense that God has given us the ground. When that happens, he makes even your enemies be at peace with you. You have favour from surrounding people and businesses. The atmosphere of the Holy Spirit can be sensed.

Sometimes you need to stand firm against the opposition in order to break through. I recall one city centre that was thick with oppression and the people tried to force us away. It took about half an hour of praise, and declaring the power of God before the atmosphere began to shift and people's hearts began to change. Two of our loudest and most aggressive hecklers changed by the time we were finished. One of them, an angry busker, came and apologised for being so unreasonable for demanding that we leave. Another man who was shouting at us broke down in tears and hugged us and thanked us for spending some time with him and giving him hope. Street ministry is warfare, and we need the anointing if we hope to be effective.

Jesus has promised you his anointing. As you see his vision, feel his heartbeat, and obey his call to go to the streets, you will experience his anointing.

FINAL THOUGHTS: HEAR THE CALL, FEEL THE CALL, OBEY THE CALL

"Not called!" did you say? "Not heard the call," I think you should say. Put your ear down to the Bible, and hear Him bid you go and pull sinners out of the fire of sin. Put your ear down to the burdened, agonized heart of humanity, and listen to its pitiful wail for help. Go stand by the gates of hell, and hear the damned entreat you to go to their father's house and bid their brothers and sisters and servants and masters not to come there. Then look Christ in the face – whose mercy you have professed to obey – and tell Him whether you will join heart and soul and body and circumstances in the march to publish His mercy to the world. – William Booth

Street preaching should never be loquacious, and I feel a book on street preaching (at least this book) should follow the same principle. The streets are not the place for lengthy sermons. The streets are the place for short, sharp and simple sound bites. You have a limited time to catch your hearer's attention. You need to get to the heart of the matter, and you need to get there quickly.

I feel this book must do the same thing. Its purpose is to get to the heart of the reader and to get there swiftly. The Lord is coming back soon. We don't know when. But the King is returning. On that

Day, there will be both great joy and great despair. Great despair for those who have not received him, and great joy for those who have. You and I are called to prepare for that Day. We are not only called to prepare ourselves, we are called to prepare others. We must go to the highways and byways and compel people to get ready because Jesus is coming.

You may think that sounds bonkers. *Is that message not outdated? Is that not the stuff of yester-year? We are more sophisticated today.* I'm not so sure. There have always been mockers. All I can say is that the Holy Spirit has so impressed the Word of God on my spirit that I believe it to be true. Therefore, if I truly believe the gospel, I am bound to proclaim this gospel to others too. (Why would I want to keep it to myself? It is the best news this world will ever hear.)

We are called to reach people, and the streets are filled with people – why would we not take the hope of Christ to the streets? We live on streets, our churches are located on streets, and daily we walk through streets – how can we remain unaffected when so many lost people walk past us every day? Lord, soften our hearts and open our eyes to see that the streets are ripe for harvest!

"The harvest is plentiful, but the laborers are few. Therefore pray earnestly to the Lord of the harvest to send out laborers into his harvest." (Luke 10:2)

APPENDICES

One of the greatest inspirations for evangelism, in my early years as a Christian, came from the revivalists and evangelists of the past. In order to help stir the fire in your belly, I've included two messages in the Appendices. I pray these messages are a blessing to your spirit, and that through them, God imparts something of the soul winning fire that these giants carried.

APPENDIX 1: "A VISION OF THE LOST" BY WILLIAM BOOTH

On one of my recent journeys, as I gazed from the coach window, I was led into a train of thought concerning the condition of the multitudes around me. They were living carelessly in the most open and shameless rebellion against God, without a thought for their eternal welfare. As I looked out of the window, I seemed to see them all... millions of people all around me given up to their drink and their pleasure, their dancing and their music, their business and their anxieties, their politics and their troubles. Ignorant- wilfully ignorant in many cases- and in other instances knowing all about the truth and not caring at all. But all of them, the whole mass of them, sweeping on and up in their blasphemies and devilries to the Throne of God. While my mind was thus engaged, I had a vision.

I saw a dark and stormy ocean. Over it the black clouds hung heavily; through them every now and then vivid lightening flashed and loud thunder rolled, while the winds moaned, and the waves rose and foamed, towered and broke, only to rise and foam, tower and break again.

In that ocean I thought I saw myriads of poor human beings plunging and floating, shouting and shrieking, cursing and struggling and drowning; and as they cursed and screamed they rose and shrieked again, and then some sank to rise no more.

And I saw out of this dark angry ocean, a mighty rock that rose up with its summit towering high above the black clouds that overhung the stormy sea. And all around the base of this great rock I saw a vast platform. Onto this platform, I saw with delight a number of the poor struggling, drowning wretches continually climbing out of the angry ocean. And I saw that a few of those who were already safe on the platform were helping the poor creatures still in the angry waters to reach the place of safety.

On looking more closely I found a number of those who had been rescued, industriously working and scheming by ladders, ropes, boats and other means more effective, to deliver the poor strugglers out of the sea. Here and there were some who actually jumped into the water, regardless of the consequences in their passion to "rescue the perishing." And I hardly know which gladdened me the most- the sight of the poor drowning people climbing onto the rocks reaching a place of safety, or the devotion and self-sacrifice of those whose whole being was wrapped up in the effort for their deliverance.

As I looked on, I saw that the occupants of that platform were quite a mixed company. That is, they were divided into different "sets" or classes, and they occupied themselves with different pleasures and employments. But only a very few of them seemed to make it their business to get the people out of the sea.

But what puzzled me most was the fact that though all of them had been rescued at one time or another from the ocean, nearly everyone seemed to have forgotten all about it. Anyway, it seemed the memory of its darkness and danger no longer troubled them at all. And what seemed equally strange and perplexing to me was that these people did not even seem to have any care- that is any agonizing care- about the poor perishing ones who were struggling and drowning right before their very eyes... many of whom were their own husbands and wives, brothers and sisters and even their own children.

Now this astonishing unconcern could not have been the result of ignorance or lack of knowledge, because they lived right there in full sight of it all and even talked about it sometimes. Many even went regularly to hear lectures and sermons in which the awful state of these poor drowning creatures was described.

I have always said that the occupants of this platform were engaged in different pursuits and pastimes. Some of them were absorbed day and night in trading and business in order to make gain, storing up their savings in boxes, safes and the like.

Many spent their time in amusing themselves with growing flowers on the side of the rock, others in painting pieces of cloth or in playing music, or in dressing themselves up in different styles and walking about to be admired. Some occupied themselves chiefly in eating and drinking, others were taken up with arguing about the poor drowning creatures that had already been rescued.

But the thing to me that seemed the most amazing was that those on the platform to whom He called, who heard His voice and felt that they ought to obey it- at least they said they did- those who confessed to love Him much were in full sympathy with Him in the task He had undertaken- who worshipped Him or who professed to do so- were so taken up with their trades and professions, their money saving and pleasures, their families and circles, their religions and arguments about it, and their preparation for going to the mainland, that they did not listen to the cry that came to them from this Wonderful Being who had Himself gone down into the sea. Anyway, if they heard it they did not heed it. They did not care. And so the multitude went on right before them struggling and shrieking and drowning in the darkness.

And then I saw something that seemed to me even more strange than anything that had gone on before in this strange vision. I saw that some of these people on the platform whom this Wonderful Being had called to, wanting them to come and help Him in His difficult task of saving these perishing creatures, were always praying and crying out to Him to come to them!

Some wanted Him to come and stay with them,

and spend His time and strength in making them happier. Others wanted Him to come and take away various doubts and misgivings they had concerning the truth of some letters He had written them. Some wanted Him to come and make them feel more secure on the rock- so secure that they would be quite sure that they should never slip off again into the ocean. Numbers of others wanted Him to make them feel quite certain that they would really get off the rock and onto the mainland someday: because as a matter of fact, it was well known that some had walked so carelessly as to lose their footing, and had fallen back again into the stormy waters.

So these people used to meet and get up as high on the rock as they could, and looking towards the mainland (where they thought the Great Being was) they would cry out, "Come to us! Come and help us!" And all the while He was down (by His Spirit) among the poor struggling, drowning creatures in the angry deep, with His arms around them trying to drag them out, and looking up- oh! so longingly but all in vain- to those on the rock, crying to them with His voice all hoarse from calling, "Come to Me! Come, and help Me!"

And then I understood it all. It was plain enough. The sea was the ocean of life- the sea of real, actual human existence. That lightening was the gleaming of piercing truth coming from Jehovah's Throne. That thunder was the distant echoing of the wrath of God. Those multitudes of people shrieking, struggling and agonizing in the stormy sea, was the thousands and thousands of poor harlots and harlot-makers, of drunkards and drunkard makers, of thieves, liars, blasphemers and ungodly people of every kindred, tongue and nation.

Oh what a black sea it was! And oh, what multitudes of rich and poor, ignorant and educated were there. They were all so unalike in their outward circumstances and conditions, yet all alike in one thing- all sinners before God- all held by, and holding onto, some iniquity, fascinated by some idol, the slaves of some devilish lust, and ruled by the foul fiend from the bottomless pit!

"All alike in one thing?" No, all alike in two things- not only the same in their wickedness but, unless rescued, the same in their sinking, sinking... down, down, down... to the same terrible doom. That great sheltering rock represented Calvary, the place where Jesus had died for them. And the people on it were those who had been rescued. The way they used their energies, gifts and time represented the occupations and amusements of those who professed to be saved from sin and hell- followers of the Lord Jesus Christ. The handful of fierce, determined ones, who were risking their own lives in saving the perishing were true soldiers of the cross of Jesus. That Mighty Being who was calling to them from the midst of the angry waters was the Son of God, "the same yesterday, today and forever" who is still struggling and interceding to save the dying multitudes about us from this terrible doom of damnation, and whose voice can be heard above the music, machinery, and noise of life, calling on the rescued to come and help Him save the world.

My friends in Christ, you are rescued from the waters, you are on the rock, He is in the dark sea calling on you to come to Him and help Him. Will you go? Look for yourselves. The surging sea of life, crowded with perishing multitudes rolls up to the very spot on which you stand. Leaving the vision, I now come to speak of the fact- a fact that is as real as the Bible, as real as the Christ who hung upon the cross, as real as the judgment day will be, and as real as the heaven and hell that will follow it.

Look! Don't be deceived by appearances- men and things are not what they seem. All who are not on the rock are in the sea! Look at them from the standpoint of the great White Throne, and what a sight you have! Jesus Christ, the Son of God is, through His Spirit, in the midst of this dying multitude, struggling to save them. And He is calling on you to jump into the sea- to go right away to His side and help Him in the holy strife. Will you jump? That is, will you go to His feet and place yourself absolutely at His disposal?

A young Christian once came to me, and told me that for some time she had been giving the Lord her profession and prayers and money, but now she wanted to give Him her life. She wanted to go right into the fight. In other words, she wanted to go to His assistance in the sea. As when a man from the shore, seeing another struggling in the water, takes off those outer garments that would hinder his efforts and leaps to the rescue, so will you who still linger on the bank, thinking and singing and praying about the poor perishing souls, lay aside your shame, your pride, your cares about other people's opinions, your love of ease and all the selfish loves that have kept you back for so long, and rush to the rescue of this multitude of dying men and women.

Does the surging sea look dark and dangerous? Unquestionably it is so. There is no doubt that the leap for you, as for everyone who takes it, means difficulty and scorn and suffering. For you it may mean more than this. It may mean death. He who beckons you from the sea however, knows what it will mean - and knowing, He still calls to you and bids to you to come.

You must do it! You cannot hold back. You have enjoyed yourself in Christianity long enough. You have had pleasant feelings, pleasant songs, pleasant meetings, pleasant prospects. There has been much of human happiness, much clapping of hands and shouting of praises- very much of heaven on earth.

Now then, go to God and tell Him you are prepared as much as necessary to turn your back upon it all, and that you are willing to spend the rest of your days struggling in the midst of these perishing multitudes, whatever it may cost you.

You must do it. With the light that is now broken

in upon your mind and the call that is now sounding in your ears, and the beckoning hands that are now before your eyes, you have no alternative. To go down among the perishing crowds is your duty. Your happiness from now on will consist in sharing their misery, your ease in sharing their pain, your crown in helping them to bear their cross, and your heaven in going into the very jaws of hell to rescue them.

Now what will you do?

APPENDIX 2: HOW TO BECOME FISHERS OF MEN BY CHARLES SPURGEON

"Come, follow me," Jesus said, "and I will make you fishers of men."
[Matthew 4:19]

When Christ calls us by his grace we must not only remember what we are, but **we must also *think of what he can make us into.***

Jesus said, "Follow me, and *I will make you*." We must repent of what we have been, and rejoice in what we may become. It is not "Follow me, because of what you already are." It is not "Follow me, because you may make something of yourselves;" but, rather, "Follow me, because of what I will make you." Truly, I might say of each one of us, as soon as we are converted, "...what we will be has not yet been made known..." [1 John 3:2]. It did not seem a likely thing that lowly fishermen would develop into apostles; that men so skillful with the fishing net would be quite as much at home in preaching sermons and instructing converts. One would have said, "How can these things be? You cannot make founders of churches out of peasants of Galilee." That is exactly what Christ did; and when we are humbled in the sight of God by a sense of our own unworthiness, we can feel encouraged to follow Jesus because of what he can make us into. What said the woman of a sorrowful spirit when she lifted up her song? "He raises the poor from the dust and lifts the needy from the ash heap; he seats them with princes..." [1 Samuel 2:8] We cannot know what God may make of us in the new creation. Who could have imagined all the beautiful things that came out from darkness and chaos by that one command, "Let there be light?" And who can tell what lovely displays of everything that is divinely pleasing may yet appear from a person's formerly dark life, when God's grace has said to them, "Let there be light?" Oh, you who presently see in yourselves nothing that is desirable, come and follow Christ for the sake of what he can make out of you. Don't you hear his sweet voice calling to you, and saying, "Follow me, and I will make you fishers of men?"

Note, next, that *we are not yet made everything that we will be,* nor everything that we should desire to be, when we were first fished for and caught. This is what the grace of God does for us at first; but it is not all. We are like the fishes, making sin to be our element; and the good Lord comes, and with the gospel net he catches us, and he delivers us from the life and love of sin. But he has not done for us all that he can do, nor all that we would wish him to do, when he has done this; for it is another and a greater miracle to make us who were fish to become fishers—to make the saved ones saviors—to make the convert into a converter—the receiver of the gospel into an imparter of that same gospel to other people.

I think I can say to every one of you—If you are already saved, then the work is only half done until you are active in bringing others to Christ. You are as yet only half formed into the image of your Lord. You have not attained to the full development of the Christ-like life in you unless you have begun in some feeble way to tell to others of the grace of God: and I trust that you will find no rest to the sole of your foot until you have been the means of leading many to that blessed Savior who is your confidence and your hope. His word is—"Follow me," not merely that you may be saved, nor even that you may be sanctified; but, "Follow me, and I will make you fishers of men." Be following Christ with that intent and aim; and fear that you are not perfectly following him, unless in some degree he is making use of you to be fishers of men.

The fact is, that every one of us must be about the business of a catching men and women for Christ. If Christ has caught us, we must catch others. If we have been apprehended of him, we must be his sheriffs, to apprehend rebels for him. Let us ask Christ to give us grace to go fishing, and have the ability to cast our nets that we may capture a great multitude of fishes. Oh that the Holy Spirit may raise up from among us some master-fishers, who will sail their boats in many seas, and surround great schools of fish!

My teaching at this time will be very simple, but I hope it will be highly practical; for my longing is that none of you, that loves the Lord, would be reluctant to fish for him.

May it be that all the members of this church, and all the Christians that hear or read this sermon are fruitful in winning the lost for Christ! The fact is, the day we live in is very dark. The heavens are lowering with heavy thunderclouds. Men often dream of what storms may soon shake this city, and the whole social fabric of this land, even to a general breaking up of society. The night is becoming so dark that the stars may seem to fall like damaged fruit from the tree. The times are evil. Now, if never before, every glow-worm or firefly must show its spark. You with the tiniest candle must take it out from under the bushel, and set it on a candlestick, where it can be seen.

We need all of you. Lot was a poor creature. He was a very, very wretched kind of believer; but still, he might have been a great blessing to Sodom had he only pleaded for the people there, as he should have done. And the weak Christians of our day, as I fear many are, need to be prayed for, for we need every one of these truly converted souls, in these evil days —Oh, let us pray that each one of them may glorify the Lord. I pray that every righteous man and woman, irritated as they are with the conversations of the wicked, may be more persistent in prayer than they has ever been, and draw near to their God, and get more spiritual life, that they might be a blessing to the people perishing all around them. I address you, therefore, at this time, first of all to dwell on this thought. Oh, that the Spirit of God may make each one of you feel your personal responsibility!

Here for believers in Christ, in the order of their usefulness, three things from our text:

1. First, *something for believers to do—Follow Jesus.* Jesus said, "Follow me."

2. Secondly, *something to be done by their great Lord and Master:* Jesus said, "...**I will make you fishers of men.**" You will not grow into fishers by yourselves, but this is what Jesus will do for you if you will just follow him.

3. **Lastly, we find** *a good illustration,* **from our great** Master; for he often spoke to the people with a parable. He presents us with an illustration of what Christians should be—*fishers of men.* We may get

some useful hints out of it, and I pray the Holy Spirit to bless them to us.

I. First, I will take it for granted that every believer here wants to be useful to Jesus. If they do not, I would question whether they could be a true believer in Christ. Well, if you want to be really useful, here is <u>SOMETHING FOR YOU TO DO TO THAT END</u>: *"Follow Jesus,* **and He will make you fishers of men."**

A young man asked, "What is the best way to become an effective preacher?" One person answers, "go to seminary." "But Christ says, "Young man, *follow me,* **and I will make you a fisher of men."** How is a person to be useful? "Attend a training-class," one says. That's true, but there is a much better answer than that—"Follow Jesus, and he will make you fishers of men." The great training school for Christian workers has Christ at its teacher; and he is at its head, not only as a tutor, but as a leader: we are not only to learn of him in study, but to follow him in action. *"Follow me,* and I will make you fishers of men." The direction is very distinct and plain, and I believe that it is exclusive, so that no one can become a fisherman by any other process. This process may appear to be very simple; but assuredly it is most effective. The Lord Jesus Christ, who knew all about fishing for men, was himself the Absolute Ruler of the rule, "Follow me, if you want to be fishers of men. If you want to be useful, follow in my steps."

1. I understand this, first, in this sense: <u>*be separated unto Christ.*</u>

These men were to leave their pursuits; they were to leave their companions; they were, in fact, to quit the world, that their one business might be, in their Master's name, to be fishers of men. *We* are not all called to leave our daily business, or to quit our families. That might be rather running away from the fishery than working at it in God's name. But we are called most distinctly to come out from among the ungodly, and to be separate, and not to touch the unclean thing. We cannot be fishers of men if we remain among men in the same element with them.

Fish will not be fishers. The sinner will not convert the sinner. The ungodly man will not convert the ungodly man; and, what is more to the point, the worldly Christian will not convert the world. If you are of the world, no doubt the world will love you as its own; but you cannot save the world. If you walk in darkness, and belong to the kingdom of darkness, you cannot remove the darkness. If you march with the armies of the wicked one, you cannot defeat them. I believe that one reason why the church of the Living God at this present moment has so little influence over the world is because the world has so much influence over the church.

Nowadays we hear Nominal and Liberal Christians insisting that they may do this and they may do that —things which their Puritan forefathers would rather have died at the stake than have tolerated. They claim that they can live like the world, and my sad answer to them, when they crave for this liberty, is, "Do it if you dare. It may not do you much more harm, for you are so bad already. Your cravings show how rotten your hearts really are. If you have a hungering after such dog food, go, you dogs, and eat the garbage. Worldly pleasures are fit food for mere pretenders and hypocrites. If you were God's children you would hate the very thought of the world's evil pleasures, and your question would not be, 'How far may we be like the world?' but your one cry would be, 'How far can we get away from the world? How much can we come out from it?'" Your desire should be to become very strict in your separation from sin, in such a time as this, than to ask, "How can I make myself like other men, and act as they do?" Brethren, the use of the church in the world is that it should be like salt in the midst of rotting; but if the salt has lost its savor, what is the good of it? If it were possible for salt itself to go bad, then it could only increase and heighten the over all rotting taking place. The worst day the world ever saw was when the sons of God were joined with the daughters of men. Then came the flood; for the only barrier against a flood of vengeance on this world is the separation of the saint from the sinner. Your duty as a Christian is to stand firm in your own place and stand out for God, hating even the clothing stained by the corrupted flesh, resolving like one of our forefathers said, "Let others do as they will, but as for us and our house, we will serve the Lord."

Come, you children of God, you must stand with your Lord outside the camp. Jesus calls to you today, and says, "Follow me." Was Jesus found at the theater? Did he frequent the sporting events or the racetracks? Do you think that Jesus was seen in any of the places of amusement and entertainment of the elite of his day? No, He was not. He was "holy, innocent, undefiled, and separate from sinners." Yet, in one sense no one mixed with sinners so completely as he did when, like a physician, he went among them healing his patients; but in another sense there was a gulf fixed between the men of the world and the Savior, which he never attempted to cross, and which they could not cross to defile him.

The first lesson which the church has to learn is this: Follow Jesus into the separated state, and he will make you fishers of men. Unless you take up your cross and protest against an ungodly world, you cannot hope that the holy Jesus will make you fishers of men.

2. A second meaning of our text is very obviously this: *live with Christ,* **and then you will be made fishers of men.**

These disciples whom Christ called were to come and live with him. They were to be associated with him every day. They were to listen to him publicly teach the eternal gospel, and in addition they were to receive special clarifications, in private, of the Word which he had spoken. They were to be his personal servants and his close friends. They were to watch his miracles and hear his prayers; and, better still, they were to be with him, and become one with him in his holy work. They were allowed to sit at the table with him, and even to have their feet washed by him. Many of them fulfilled that word, "Where you live, I will live:" they were with him in his afflictions and persecutions. They witnessed his secret agonies; they saw his many tears; they noted the passion and the compassion of his soul, and thus, in time, they caught his spirit, and so they learned to be fishers of men.

At Jesus' feet we must learn the art and mystery of soul-winning, to live with Christ is the best education for usefulness. It is a great advantage to any Christian to be associated with a Christian minister whose heart is on fire. The best training for a young man is that which a group of pastors, in the 17th century, gave, in which each elderly pastor had a young man with him who walked with him whenever he went up the mountainside to preach, and lived in the house with him, and listened to his prayers and observed his daily holiness. This was a fine instruction, was it not? But it will not compare with that of the apostles who lived with Jesus himself, and were his daily companions. Unparalleled was the training of the twelve. No wonder that they became what they were with such a heavenly tutor to saturate them with his own spirit! And now today his bodily presence is not among us; but his spiritual power is perhaps more fully known to us than it was to those apostles in those two or three years of the Lord's earthly presence. There are some of us to whom he is intimately near. We know more about him than we do about our dearest earthly friends. We have never been quite able to totally understand our dearest friend's heart in all its twists and turns, but we know the heart of the Jesus Christ. We have leaned our head upon his chest, and have enjoyed fellowship with him such as we could not have had with any of our own friends and relatives. This is the surest way of learning how to do good. Live with Jesus, follow Jesus, and he will make you fishers of men.

Watch how he does the work, and therefore learn how to do it yourself. A Christian man should be an apprentice to Jesus to learn the trade of a Savior. We can never save men by offering a redemption, for we have none to present; **but we can learn how to save men and women by warning them to flee from the wrath to come**, and setting before them the one great effective remedy. Watch how Jesus saves, and you will learn how it is done: You cannot learn it any other way. Live in fellowship with Christ, and people will notice that you have a certain demeanor about you, that seems to make you very capable to teach and to win souls.

3. A third meaning, however, must be given to this "Follow me," and it is this: *"Obey me,* **and then you will know what to do to save men."**

We must not talk about our fellowship with Christ, or our being separated from the world unto him, unless we make him our Master and Lord in everything. Some preachers are not true to all of their convictions, so how can they look for a blessing? A Christian who wants to useful to the Lord, ought to be very particular as to every point of obedience to his Master. I have no doubt whatever that God blesses our churches even when they are somewhat flawed, for his mercy endures forever. When there is a measure of error in the teaching, and a measure of mistake in the practice, he may still consent to use the ministry, for he is very gracious. But a large measure of blessing must necessarily be withheld from all teaching, which is knowingly or glaringly faulty. God can set his seal upon the truth that is in it, but he cannot set his seal upon the error that is in it. Out of mistakes about Christian ordinances and other things, especially errors in heart and spirit, there may come evils, which we never looked for. Such evils may even now be influential on the present age, and may work worse damage on future generations. If we desire as fishers of men to be largely used of God we must copy our Lord Jesus in everything, and obey him in every point. Failure in obedience may lead to failure in success. Each one of us, if he would wish to see his child saved, or his Sunday-School class blessed, or his congregation converted, must be careful that, he is a clean instrument of the Lord. Anything we do that grieves the Spirit of God must take away from us some part of our power for good. The Lord is very gracious and compassionate; but yet he is a jealous God. He is sometimes sternly jealous towards his people who are knowingly neglecting obedience to certain of his commands, or are in associations, which are not clean in his sight. He will hinder their work, weaken their strength, and humble them until they finally say, "My Lord, I will follow you after all. I will do what you call me to do, or else you will not accept me." The Lord said to his disciples, "Go into all the world and preach the good news to all creation. Whoever believes and is baptized will be saved" [Mark 16:15]. Now, we must get back to apostolic practice and to apostolic teaching: we must lay aside the commandments of men and the impulses of our own brains, and we must do what Christ tells us, as Christ tells us, and because Christ tells us. Definitely and distinctly, we must take the place of servants; and if we will not do that, we cannot expect our Lord to work with us and through us. Let us be determined that, as true as the compass needle is to the north pole, so true will we be, as far as our light goes, to the command of our Lord and Master.

Jesus says—"Follow me, and I will make you fishers of men." By this teaching he seems to say—"If you go ahead of me, or fall back behind me, and you cast the net; you will catch nothing. However, when you do as I command you, you will cast your net on the right side of the boat, and you will find a great catch."

4. Again, **I think that there is a great lesson in my**

text to those *who preach their own thoughts instead of preaching the thoughts of Christ.*

These disciples were to follow Christ that they might listen to him, hear what he had to say, drink in his teaching, and then *go and teach what he had taught them.* Their Lord says, "What I tell you in the dark, speak in the daylight; what is whispered in your ear, proclaim from the roofs" [Matthew 10:27]. If they will be faithful messengers of Christ's message, he will make them "fishers of men." But you know the proud method nowadays is this: "I am not going to preach this old, old gospel, this musty Puritan doctrine. I will sit down in my study, and burn the midnight oil, and invent a new theory; then I will come out with my brand new thought, and blaze away with it."

Many are not following Christ, but following themselves, and of them the Lord may well say, "You will see whose word will stand, mine or theirs." Others are wickedly discreet, and judge that certain truths, which are clearly God's word, had better be kept back. They say, "You must not be harsh, but must preach friendly things. To talk about the punishment of sin, to speak of eternal punishment, why, these are unfashionable doctrines. It may be that they are taught in the Word of God, but they do not suit the intellect of this age. We must trim them down."

Brothers in Christ, I will have no part of their wickedness. Will you? Our enlightened age believed that they have discovered certain things not taught in the Bible. Evolution may be clearly contrary to the teaching of Genesis, but that doesn't matter to them. They are not going to be believers of Scripture, but original thinkers. This is the arrogant ambition of the age we live in. Note this, in proportion as the modern theology is preached the depravity of this generation will increase. To a great degree I attribute the looseness of our age to the carelessness of the doctrine preached by its teachers. From the pulpit they have taught the people that sin is a small thing. From the pulpit these traitors to God and to his Christ have taught the people <u>that there is no hell to be feared</u>. A little, little hell, perhaps, there may be; but justified punishment for sin is made nothing of. The precious atoning sacrifice of Christ has been derided and misrepresented by those who were pledged to preach it. They have given the people the name of the gospel, but the gospel itself has evaporated in their hands.

From hundreds of pulpits the gospel has disappeared; and still the preachers take the position and name of Christ's ministers. Well, and what comes of it? Why, their congregations grow thinner and thinner; and so it must be. Jesus says, "Follow *me,* I will make you fishers of men;" but if you go your own way, with your own net, you will make nothing of it, and the Lord promises you no help in it. The Lord's directions makes himself our leader and example. It is:

"Follow *me,* follow *me.* Preach *my* gospel. Preach what I preached. Teach what I taught, and keep to that." Do this, and he will make you fishers of men; but if you do not do this, you will fish in vain.

5. I close this part of my discourse by saying that <u>we will not be fishers of men unless we follow Christ in one other respect; and that is, by endeavoring, in all points, to *imitate his holiness.*</u>

Holiness is the greatest real power that can be possessed by men or women. We may preach the truth, but we must also live the truth. God forbid that we should preach anything else; but it will be all in vain, unless there is a life at the back of the testimony. An unholy preacher may even render truth contemptible. In proportion as any of us draw back from a living a zealous sanctification we will draw back from the place of power. Our power lies in this word, "Follow me." Be like Jesus.

In all things endeavor to think, and speak, and act as Jesus did, and he will make you fishers of men. This will require self-denial. We must daily take up the cross. This may require willingness to give up our reputation—readiness to be thought fools, idiots, and the like, as men are apt to call those who are keeping close to their Master. There must be the cheerful resigning of everything that looks like honor and personal glory, in order that we may be completely Christ's, and glorify his name. We must live his life and be ready to die his death, if need be. O brothers and sisters, if we do this and follow Jesus, putting our feet into the footprints of his pierced feet, he will make us fishers of men. If it should so please him that we should even die without having gathered many souls to the cross, we will speak from our graves. In some way or other the Lord will make a holy life to be an influential life. It is not possible that a life, which can be described as following Christ, should be an unsuccessful one in the sight of the Most High. "Follow me," and there is an "I will" such as God can never draw back from: "Follow me, and I will make you fishers of men."

Thus much on the first point. There is something for us to do: we are graciously called to follow

Jesus. Holy Spirit, lead us to do it.

II. But secondly, and briefly, there is <u>SOMETHING FOR THE LORD TO DO.</u>

1. When his dear servants are following him, he says, "I will make you fishers of men;" and **be it never forgotten** that *it is he that makes us follow him;* so that if the following of Christ be the step to being made a fisher of men, yet this he gives us. 'It is all of his Spirit. I have talked about catching his spirit, and abiding in him, and obeying him, and listening to him, and copying him; but none of these things are we capable of apart from his working them all in us. "…your fruitfulness comes from me" [Hosea 14:8], is a text which we must not for a moment forget. So, then, if we do follow him, it is he that makes us follow him; and so he makes us fishers of men.

2. But, further, if we follow Christ <u>he will make us fishers of men</u> *by all our experience.*

I am sure that the man who is really consecrated to bless others will be helped in this by all that he feels, especially by his afflictions. I often feel very grateful to God that I have undergone fearful depression of spirits. I know the borders of despair, and the horrible brink of that gulf of darkness into which my feet have almost gone; but hundreds of times I have been able to give a helpful grip to brethren and sisters who have come into that same condition, which grip I could never have given if I had not known their deep despondency.

So I believe that the darkest and most dreadful experience of a child of God will help him to be a fisher of men if he will but follow Christ. Keep close to your

Lord and he will make every step a blessing to you. If God in providence should make you rich, he will allow you to speak to those ignorant and wicked rich who so much abound in this city, and so often are the cause of its worst sin. And if the Lord is pleased to let you be very poor you can go down and talk to those wicked and ignorant poor people who so often are the cause of sin in this city, and so greatly need the gospel. The winds of providence will move you to where you can fish for men and women. The wheels of providence are full of eyes, and all those eyes will look this way to help us to be winners of souls. You will often be surprised to find how God has been in a house that you visit: before you get there, his hand has been at work in its rooms. When you wish to speak to some particular individual, God's providence has been dealing with that individual to make him ready for just that word which you could say, but which nobody else but you could say.

Oh, be you following Christ, and you will find that he will, by every experience through which you are passing, make you fishers of men.

3. Further than that, <u>if you will follow him he will make you fishers of men</u> *by distinct warnings of impending dangers in your own heart.*

The Holy Spirit warns us of many impending dangers, which are not noticed by Christians when they are in an indifferent condition; but when the heart is right with God and living in communion with God, we feel a sacred sensitivity, so that we do not need the Lord to shout, but his faintest whisper is heard. No, he doesn't even have to whisper, and yet we hear Him.

Oh, how many willful Christians there are who must

be controlled tightly with the bit and bridle, and receive a lash of the whip every now and then! But the Christian who follows his Lord will be tenderly guided. I do not say that the Spirit of God will say to you, "Go to that chariot," or that you will hear a word in your ear; but yet in your soul, as distinctly as the Holy Spirit said to Philip, "Go to that chariot and stay near it" [Acts 8:29], you will hear the Lord's will. As soon as you see an individual, the thought will cross your mind, "Go and speak to that person." Every opportunity of usefulness will be a call to you. If you are ready, the door will open before you, and you will hear a voice behind you saying, "This is the way; walk in it." If you have the grace to run in the right way you will never be long without an inkling as to what the right way is. That right way will lead you to river or sea, where you can cast your net, and be a fisher of men.

4. Then, too, **I believe that the Lord meant by this that** *he would give his followers the Holy Spirit.*

They were to follow him, and then, when they had seen him ascend into the clouds, to the holy place of the Most High, they were to stay in Jerusalem for a little while, and the Holy Spirit would come upon them and clothe them with power from on high [Luke 24:49]. This word was spoken to Peter and Andrew; and you know how it was fulfilled to Peter. What a multitude of fish he brought to land the first time he threw his net in the power of the Holy Spirit! [John 21:6]. "Follow me, and I will make you fishers of men."

Brothers and sisters, we have no conception of what God could do through this congregation of believers gathered in our Church tonight. If right now, we

STREETS RIPE FOR HARVEST

were to be filled with the Holy Spirit, there are enough of us here, to evangelize our entire city. There are enough here to be the means of the salvation of the world. Let us seek a blessing; and if we seek it let us hear his guiding voice, "Follow me, and I will make you fishers of men."

You men and women that sit before me today, you are sitting by the shore of a great sea of human life swarming with the souls of men and women. You live in the midst of millions; but if you will follow Jesus, and be faithful to him, and true to him, and do what he commands you to do, he will make you fishers of men.

Do not say, "Who will save this city?" The weakest will be strong enough. Samson, with a fresh jawbone of a donkey, taken up from the earth where it was lying bleaching in the sun, killed a thousand Philistines [Judges 15:15-16]. Do not fear, nor be dismayed. Let your responsibilities drive you closer to your Master. Let the shock of the prevailing sins of our land make you look into his dear face who long ago wept over Jerusalem, and now weeps over our cities. Take hold of Christ, and never let him go. By the strong and mighty impulses of the divine life within you, quickened and brought to maturity by the Holy Spirit of God, learn this lesson from your Lord's own mouth: "Follow me, and I will make you fishers of men."

You are not fit for such a task, but he will make you fit. You cannot do it by yourselves, but he will make you do it. You do not know how to spread the nets and draw schools of fish to shore, but he will teach you. Only follow him, and he will make you fishers of men.

I wish that I could somehow say this as with a voice of thunder, that the whole church of God on earth might hear it. I wish I could write it in stars diagonally across the sky, "Jesus said, Follow me, and I will make you fishers of men." If you forget the edict, the promise will never be yours. If you follow some other track, or imitate some other leader, you will fish in vain. God grant us to believe fully that Jesus can do great things in us, and then do great things by us for the good of all those around us!

III. The last point you might study in your private meditations with much benefit. We have here AN ILLUSTRATION FULL OF INSTRUCTION. I will give you a few thoughts which you can use. "I will make you *fishers of men.*" You have been fishers of fish: if you follow me, I will make you fishers of men.

1. A fisher is a person who is *very dependent, and needs to have faith.*

He cannot see the fish. One who fishes in the sea must go and throw in the net, as it were, at an uncertain possibility. Fishing is an act of faith. I have often seen in the Mediterranean men go with their boats and enclose acres of sea with vast nets; and yet, when they have drawn the net to shore, they have not had even a whole handful of fish. A few wretched silvery nothings have made up the whole catch. Yet they have gone again and thrown the great net several times a day, hopefully expecting something to come of it.

Nobody is so dependent upon God as a minister of God. Oh, this fishing from the Church's pulpit! What a work of faith! I cannot tell that a soul will be brought to God by it. I cannot judge whether my sermon will be suitable to the persons who are here, except that I do believe that God will guide me in the throwing of the net. I expect him to work salvation, and I depend upon him for it. I love this complete dependence, and if I could be offered a certain amount of preaching power, by which I could save sinners, which should be entirely at my own disposal, I would beg the Lord not to let me have it, for it is far more delightful to be entirely dependent upon him at all times. It is a blessed thing to be weak if Christ becomes more fully your strength. Go to work, you who would be fishers of men, and yet feel your insufficiency. You that have no strength, attempt this divine work. Your Master's strength will be seen when your own strength is gone. A fisherman is a dependent person, he must look up for success every time he puts the net down; but still he is a person of faith, and therefore he throws in the net joyfully.

2. A fisherman who makes his living by fishing is *a diligent and persevering man*.

The fishers are up at dawn. At daybreak our fishermen are fishing, and they continue fishing till late in the afternoon. As long as hands can work men will fish. May the Lord Jesus make us hard working, persevering, unwearied fishers of men! "Sow your seed in the morning, and at evening time do not let your hands be idle, for you do not know which will succeed, whether this or that..." [Ecclesiastes 11:6].

3. The skillful fisherman is *intelligent and watchful*.

It looks very easy, I dare say, to be a fisherman, but you would find that it was no child's play if you were to take a real part in it. There is an art in it, from the mending of the net right on to the pulling it to shore.

How diligent the fisherman must be to prevent the fish from leaping out of the net! I heard a great noise one night in the sea, as if a giant was beating some huge drum; and I looked out, and I saw that the fishermen were beating the water to drive the fish into the net, or to keep them from leaping out of it, while the net was being closed around them. Ah, yes! And you and I will often have to be watching the corners of the gospel net lest sinners who are almost caught should make their escape. They are very crafty, these fish, and they use this craftiness in endeavoring to avoid salvation. We will have to be always at our business, and to exercise all our faculties, and more than our own intellects, if we are to be successful fishers of men.

4. The fisherman is *a very hard working person*.

Being a fisherman is not an easy calling. He does not sit in an armchair and catch fish. He often has to go out in harsh weather. If a farmer worries about the clouds he will never sow, likewise, a fisherman that worries about the clouds will never fish. If we never do any work for Christ except when we feel up to it, then we will not do much. If we feel that we will not pray because we cannot pray, we will never pray, and if we say, "I will not preach today because I do not feel that I could preach," we will never preach any preaching that is worth the preaching. We must be always at it, until we wear ourselves out, throwing our whole soul into the work in all circumstances, for Christ's sake.

5. The fisherman is *a daring man*.

He tempts the boisterous sea. A little brine in his face does not hurt him; he has been wet through a thousand times, it is nothing to him. He never expected when he became a deep-sea fisherman that he was going to sleep in the lap of comfort. So the true minister of Christ who fishes for souls will never mind a little risk. He will be bound to do or say many a thing that is very unpopular; and some Christian people may even judge his words to be too severe. He must do and say that which is for the good of souls. It is not his to entertain a question as to what others will think of his doctrine, or of him; but in the name of the Almighty God he must feel, "If the sea thunders and crashes, still at my Master's command I will let down the net."

6. Now, in the last place, the man whom Christ makes a fisher of men *is successful*.

"But," one says, "I have always heard that Christ's ministers are to be faithful, but that they cannot be sure of being successful." Yes, I have heard that saying too, and in one way I know it is true, but in another way I have my doubts about it. He that is faithful is, in God's way and in God's judgment, more or less successful.

For instance, here is a brother who says that he is faithful. Of course, I must believe him, yet I never heard of a sinner being saved under his ministry. Indeed, I would think that the safest place for a person to be in if he did not want to be saved would be under this gentleman's ministry, because he does not preach anything that is likely to arouse, impress, or convince anybody. This brother is "faithful:" so he says.

So likewise, if any person in the world said to you, "I am a fisherman, but I have never caught anything," you would wonder how he could be called a fisherman. A farmer who never grew any wheat, or any other crop—is he a farmer? When Jesus Christ says, "Follow me, and I will make you fishers of men," he means, that you will, really catch men and women—that you really, will save some; for he that never did catch any fish is not a fisherman. He that never saved a sinner after years of work is not a minister of Christ. If the result of his life work is *nothing,* he made a mistake when he undertook it. Go with the fire of God in your hand and fling it among the straw, and the straw will burn. You can be sure of that. Go and scatter the good seed: it may not all fall in fertile places, but some of it will. You can be sure of that. Go and let your light shine, and someone's eye will see the light. You must, you will succeed. But remember this is the Lord's word—"Follow me, and I will make you fishers of men." Keep close to Jesus, and do as Jesus did, in his spirit, and he will make you fishers of men.

Conclusion

Perhaps I speak to an attentive hearer who is not converted at all.

Friend, I have the same thing to say to you. You may also follow Christ, and then he can use you, even you. I don't know but that he has brought you to this place that you may be saved, and that in years to come he may make you speak for his name and glory. Remember how he called Saul of Tarsus, and made him the apostle to the Gentiles. Recovered poachers make the best gamekeepers; and saved sinners make the most capable preachers.

Oh, that you would run away from your old master, Satan, tonight, without giving him a minute's notice; for if you give him any notice, he will hold on to you. Rush to Jesus, and say, "Here I am a poor runaway slave! My Lord, I bear the shackles still upon my wrists. Will you set me free, and make me your own?" Remember, it is written, "...whoever comes to me I will never drive away" [John 6:37]. Never did a runaway slave come to Christ in the middle of the night without Jesus taking him in; and he never gave one up back to his old master. If Jesus makes you free you will be free indeed. Quickly flee to Jesus. May the Holy Spirit help you, and he will in time make you a winner of others to his praise! God bless you. Amen.

Printed in Great Britain
by Amazon